Pride and Protest
The Novel in Indiana

A LITERARY MAP OF INDIANA

Other Hoosier Writers

David Wolf Anderson
John D. Barnhart
Charles Austin Beard
Mary Ritter Beard
Clarence Benadum
Horace Peter Biddle
Claude Bowers
Rollo Walter Brown
Margaret E. Bruner
R. Carlyle Buley
William J. Cuppy
Julia Louisa Cory Dumont
Jacob Piatt Dunn
Maurice Francis Egan
Logan Esarey
Strickland Gillilan
Elizabeth Jane Miller Hack
Holman Hamilton
Bertita Leonarz Harding
William Herschell
McCready Huston
John T. McCutcheon
Sister Mary Madeleva
James G. Randall
Solon Robinson
Charles Elbert Scoggins
Henry Thew Stephenson
Jessamyn West
Kenneth P. Williams
Forceythe Willson
Marguerite Young

Other Writers for Younger People

John Barton Gruelle
Mabel Leigh Hunt
Clara Ingram Judson
Janet Lambert
Laura Long
Jeannette Covert Nolan

PREPARED JOINTLY BY
The Indiana Council of Teachers of English
The Indiana College English Association
Copyright 1956

The Committee: Chairman, Seward S. Craig;
Ruth B. Bacelt, Arthur W. Shumaker, William A. Bufkin;
Esther Thornton, George S. Wykoff, Ex officio; Mary L. Otten,
President, ICTE; and Elijah L. Jacobs, President, ICEA.
The Artist: Warren Causs, Ball State Teachers College.

Principal Sources: R.E. Banta; INDIANA AUTHORS and HOOSIER CARAVAN;
A.W. Shumaker, Doctoral Dissertation, A LITERARY HISTORY OF INDIANA;
The Indiana Library Association, The Indiana State Library, Public
Library of Indianapolis, The Indiana Historical Society.
Appreciation is due hundreds of teachers, librarians, literary
and historical society members and other interested persons
who graciously advised the committee.

Criteria of Inclusion
The writers here represented are identified with Indiana and
its culture. All, native or adopted, have concerned themselves with
Indiana people and scenes or have brought distinction to the state
through their imaginative or artistic literature—and, in a few
instances, history.

A HOOSIER BOOKSHELF

Order from Seward S. Craig, Chairman, Thomas Carr Howe High School. Indianapolis, Indiana. $1.50 postpaid.

Pride and Protest
The Novel in Indiana

JEANETTE VANAUSDALL

Indiana Historical Society
Indianapolis 1999

Printed in the United States of America

The paper in this publication meets the minimum requirements of American National Standard for Information Sciences—Permanence of Paper for Printed Library Materials, ANSI Z39.48–1984

Library of Congress Cataloging-in-Publication Data

Vanausdall, Jeanette.
   Pride and protest : the novel in Indiana / Jeanette Vanausdall.
     p.   cm.
   Includes bibliographical references and index.
   ISBN 0-87195-134-7 (cloth : acid-free paper)
    1. American fiction–Indiana–History and criticism. 2. Indiana--Intellectual life. 3. Indiana–In literature. I. Title.
PS283.I6V36 1999
813.009'9772–dc21
                                      99-23984
                                        CIP

To my grandfather, Seward S. Craig, a Hoosier schoolmaster

Contents

Preface

This book is not a comprehensive overview of Indiana literature; that has been done ably, however long ago, by Arthur W. Shumaker. Neither is it the standard discussion of the golden age authors that can be found in any chapter on Indiana literary history. It will not revisit the too-familiar literary facts, figures, and anecdotes to which Hoosiers have become so accustomed and, I might add, inadvertently attached.

It is my opinion that we diminish Indiana literature by focusing so intensely on Hoosier literary trivia, and we betray a certain lack of sophistication by continually showcasing the so-called golden age, a short-lived, essentially unexplainable phenomenon, the literary equivalent of our fifteen minutes of fame. Therefore, this book will not discuss what real Indianapolis residence was the probable prototype of the Amberson mansion, for example, or exactly what county is represented by Hoopole. Above all, this book will discontinue the time-honored tradition of attempting to make a case for how we distinguish ourselves. Instead, this book will seek to show how we fit within the broader context of American literature, which should be a source of pride.

In preparing this book I continually asked myself what I might tell someone from Oklahoma or Connecticut about Indiana literature that might inspire that person to read some of it. What aspects of Indiana fiction would resonate enough with any reader to cause him or her to want to explore it? What are the enduring themes in American literature that are represented by exemplary Hoosier fiction? What are the major schools, movements, or genres in American literature to which Hoosiers have contributed?

In the attempt to put Indiana literature in perspective I have chosen the form of the novel because it is through the novel that Indiana has distinguished itself, to whatever degree it has, in American literature. It is the novel that has defined American literature since the Civil War. It is the novel that dominated, with the exception of Riley's poetry, Indiana's golden age. I also include selected short fiction because the short story was formative for many novelists and because it figures prominently in Indiana literature.

In the interest of setting Indiana fiction within the broader context of American literature, I have concentrated on distinct movements in American fiction and on how Indiana has represented itself within those movements. Therefore I have been forced to leave out some commendable works by competent writers either because they did not reflect those formative literary movements or because they were not written by authors of the periods under discussion, but by skilled authors of a later time who simply treated the same subject matter. Leroy MacLeod, for example, wrote in the 1930s about life on an Indiana farm immediately following the Civil War; he is included because he was a farm novelist at the height of the era of production and popularity of farm fiction, and because his work is particularly meritorious. Don Kurtz, author of *South of the Big Four*, an excellent contemporary farm novel set in Indiana, does not figure in the rural fiction chapter because he wrote after the period. Also, some beloved and talented writers such as Jessamyn West and Margaret Weymouth Jackson do not figure as prominently as some admirers might like because their works did not fit neatly into clearly defined movements or representative subject matter.

Likewise contemporary authors have been treated rather summarily, not because of any judgment about the enduring quality of their work or their merit as Indiana authors, but simply because it will be for future generations to judge their lasting place in the literary movements of our time. Short story writers such as Susan Neville and Michael Martone merit discussion in the chapter on contemporary authors because they have distinguished themselves in the current vogue of writing about place, while some other authors such as James Alexander Thom and Nancy N. Baxter, who write quality historical fiction for today's market and who may well merit examination by future generations, do not fit that description. Talented writers such as Daryl Pinckney, Elizabeth Arthur, or Lisa Vice, who have earned the praise of critics and merit the attention of every literate Hoosier as well, also have not entered into this discussion as much as some readers might like, either because their work has been set elsewhere or, though set in Indiana, has not been sufficiently about Indiana or influenced by Indiana to serve the purposes of this study.

I have chosen fiction that speaks to us in some profound and fundamental way of Indiana because I am convinced that it is only in regional setting and subject matter that a state's literary heritage truly reveals itself. In the introduction to *Native Folk Spirit in Literature*, a collection of essays by Maurice Thompson, Meredith Nicholson, and Hamlin Garland, editor J. Christian Bays writes that "the spirit of a people is understood best by a study of that people's literature."[1]

I come by my interest in Indiana literature honestly. My grandfather, Seward S. Craig, longtime chairman of the English department at Thomas Carr Howe High School in Indianapolis, served as chairman of a committee that produced a fine literary map of Indiana in 1956. Created jointly by the Indiana Council of Teachers of English and the Indiana College English Association, the committee included the likes of Arthur W. Shumaker, author of *A History of Indiana Literature*. My grandfather's copy of the map hung in his study until he died in 1988, and it now hangs in what passes for my office. The map was as much a fixture of my childhood as his ancient Corona typewriter—the permanent impression of his thumb on the space bar—and the smell of his pipe smoke. I run across the map every now and then in antique shops. My grandmother, also a teacher and a voracious reader, was in love with the popular literature of Indiana and, as a young Minnesotan woman being courted by my grandfather, referred to him proudly in letters and diary as "the gentleman from Indiana" and "the Hoosier schoolmaster."

The map includes in the credits a paragraph entitled "Criteria of Inclusion." It reads: "The writers here represented are identified with Indiana and its culture. All, native or adopted, have concerned themselves with Indiana people or scenes or have brought distinction to the state through their imaginative or artistic literature—and, in a few instances, history." While this seems to be as succinct and thoughtful a set of criteria as any I have read, I have chosen not to enter into a general discussion of what constitutes an Indiana author. Each author's inclusion in this book will be discussed and, I hope, justified, in his or her respective chapter.

All these disclaimers have served to limit the scope of the book, and therefore, I am aware, a certain degree of culpability for exclusions and omissions. But it should be noted that the subject of Indiana literature is so vast that no one could ever claim to have read, much less written thoughtfully about, all of it. When I began this project, I suffered under the illusion that I could find and read every work of fiction set in Indiana, written by any author, Hoosier or otherwise. Though I have read more than two hundred novels and short stories, many several times over, I am painfully aware that I have not read everything.

More realistically, I entertained the hope that I could hold up for attention some under-read, but worthy, works or authors who deserve new or more exposure. In fact, the majority of novels and story collections that I considered for this project had to be read in libraries because they are long out of print and cannot circulate or be purchased. The Indianapolis–Marion County Public Library keeps many of them in a vault. Some still bear the old cards that show them having last been checked out in the 1930s or 1940s. I still nurse the hope that I might inspire at least a handful of Hoosier readers to seek them out and enjoy them.

I would like to acknowledge the assistance of many individuals and institutions, foremost of them Peter T. Harstad and the Indiana Historical Society, and particularly the Clio committee for making this kind of research possible to writers of Indiana history. I would like to acknowledge the encouragement, insight, and wise counsel of Robert M. Taylor, Jr., of the Society and J. Kent Calder, formerly of that institution. I would like to thank Paula Corpuz, Shirley McCord, Kathy Breen, and George Hanlin of the Publications Division of the Indiana Historical Society for their editing and patience and the staff of the Society's William Henry Smith Memorial Library, a patron-friendly and knowledgeable staff.

In addition I would like to thank the staff of the Indiana State Library, particularly Dave Lewis, and Dr. Ronald Dehnke of Indiana University–Purdue University at Columbus for reading and commenting upon several chapters of this manuscript.

Finally, but by no means least or last in my gratitude, I would like to thank my parents, husband, and children who helped me make the time and find the energy for this project and the many friends who offered to entertain my children during the course of my work and who inquired about it regularly and encouraged me.

Introduction

Between the years 1870 and 1920 Indiana novelists produced a disproportionate number of best-sellers. The significance of that fact to the history of American literature is subject to debate.

Historians of the state have devoted much energy to analyzing the literary phenomenon of Indiana's golden age, and still it defies explanation. One problem is that of the numerous theories posited to account for the state's literary "prominence," none of them applies uniquely to Indiana. Whether it was the influence of frontier isolation and illiteracy that may have encouraged a rich tradition of storytelling and native folklore, or the later appearance of literary societies, libraries, universities, and publishing houses in the larger cities, Indiana's neighboring states experienced the same set of circumstances.

Hoosiers like to point to a diverse population that incorporated elements of both the South and New England in its culture, but that blending of cultures is shared by their immediate neighbors, particularly Ohio and Illinois. Indiana's supposed love affair with politics and its wealth of newspapers is claimed by its bordering states as well.

Read the introduction to *Ohio Authors and Their Books*, edited by William Coyle, *Writing Illinois: The Prairie, Lincoln, and Chicago*, by James Hurt, or Robert C. Bray's *Rediscoveries: Literature and Place in Illinois*. Substitute the word Indiana for Ohio or Illinois in any of them and you might think you were reading about the literary heritage of the Hoosier State.

Hurt speaks of the literature of Illinois having been influenced by the "flatness of the landscape," and by the "provinciality of the culture," of literature that has been at times little more than "hollow boosterism . . . that betray[s] a nervous defensiveness."[1]

Coyle discusses legitimate claims to an Ohio literature "inclined toward the sentimental, the moralistic."[2] He mentions "a decided proclivity for humor" and a "considerable responsiveness to public taste" among Ohio authors. Most demoralizing of all for proud Hoosiers, he suggests that "one of the proudest boasts of

Ohioans is that they live in the typical American state, the epitome of average America."[3] Coyle is careful to point out that none of these characteristics is the exclusive property of Ohio authors, that they are probably aspects of all midwestern literature, but it does not soften the blow. Hoosiers like to think that Indiana stands out among midwestern states in some fashion, and some historians have latched onto its literary reputation with an inordinate tenacity.

Indiana noticeably lacks writers of the caliber and critical regard of its fellow midwestern states. It can boast of none comparable to a William Dean Howells or a Sherwood Anderson, a Sinclair Lewis or a Willa Cather. Indiana also lacks a unifying subject matter such as that which James Hurt claims for Illinois. "The more Illinois texts I read," he writes, "the more I become aware of how much the sense of place in Illinois has been formed around the fact of the prairie landscape, the memory of Lincoln, and the presence of Chicago."[4]

Has Indiana anything comparable in the way of literary "centers" or landscapes? There are two or three lackluster novels about the New Harmony experiment and a handful of novels about Morgan's Raid, none of them memorable. There is no significant literature of the 500-Mile Race or the automobile in Indiana. The state can boast of no mythic figure like a Lincoln (though we claim a small piece of him) or no city of the stature of Chicago that has inspired its own literature. There is no Hoosier "school" in that sense.

In fact, the only thing unique about Indiana's literary history is that there seems to have been a "community" of writers at the turn of the century that knew each other, liked each other, and supported and encouraged each other in their work to a degree not experienced in the other midwestern states. There is the added phenomenon that so many Indiana authors lived out their lives in Indiana. Indeed, there have been perhaps more writers who have lived in Indiana than there have been writers from Indiana. So perhaps it could be said that there was a Hoosier literary "community," if not a school. While that happy fact is nothing to dismiss, it hardly substitutes for a distinct Hoosier "voice."

The golden age really belongs to the Midwest as a region. The very period that Hoosiers claim as their golden age of literature, approximately from 1870 to 1920, was in fact the golden age of the entire Midwest in terms of economic development, of urbanization, of industrialization, of literacy, and of the rise of an educated middle class with leisure time to read. In addition, and not coincidentally, it was the golden age of publishing and of the novel as the new and preferred literary form.

It would seem that Hoosiers in their exuberance have made something of a golden calf of the golden age, and in doing so have distracted and shortchanged themselves. By trying so hard to set themselves apart, Hoosiers have ignored what makes them a part of the greater glory of American literature.

That glory is best characterized by the expression of the idea of America itself, of America as the new frontier, the new Eden, and of the American frontiersman as the new man. As the frontier pushed west, so too did the desire to express, through literature, a brand-new experience, to extol the wonders of a vast new landscape, as well as to despair of its resistance to human settlement.

Wilson O. Clough in *The Necessary Earth: Nature and Solitude in American Literature* writes that "a native literature must be born of wrestling with the direct and native experience as against a literature derivative merely from the past."[5] This sentiment perhaps best explains the appearance of regional literature in the American literary landscape. Each new experience marked a departure from the literary influences of Europe and New England because each successive frontier represented a new and unique opportunity to rediscover or reclaim the promise of the New World.

In one way or another all of American literature has been a story of struggling against or within the physical environment, be it the untamed wilderness of the frontier or the urban jungle. There is an American literature of mountain, of desert, and of river. In *The Role of Place in Literature*, Leonard Lutwack writes that it is sometimes "difficult to avoid the proposition that in the final analysis all places in literature are used for symbolical purposes even though in their descriptiveness they may be rooted in fact."[6] Has Indiana, then, been more than just a setting as good as any other to tell a story? What has Indiana as a distinct *place* symbolized in American literature?

CHAPTER ONE

Moral Geography

The Great Forest and the Frontier Experience

Simply because of its geography Indiana does not lend itself to a literature of mountain, desert, sea, or, with a few notable exceptions, river. It is not represented by a folklore of enduring geophysical symbolism, of defining landscapes that stand the test of time and the vagaries of human history. Indiana, and much of the Midwest, has been blessed with a more fragile and transitory topography, one that has been more affected by human settlement than perhaps other regions. Indeed, the most pervasive imagery that appears in Indiana lore and literature is forest imagery, and the vast primeval forest that once covered the Indiana Territory has all but disappeared.

Frontier Indiana lay enshrouded in one of the largest deciduous hardwood forests in the world, and the frontiersmen who dared enter it shared one common and formative experience—that of being swallowed. The great forest stretched as far as the eye could see and the untutored imagination could envision, about twenty million acres of primeval forest in the Indiana Territory alone, nearly ten times the area of prairie or wetlands.[1] It was virtually impenetrable. A settler could travel for days under a canopy so thick it blotted out the sun and muffled all extraneous sound.

Burial imagery is a common theme in Indiana literature. Countless images of darkness, death, shade, solitude, and stillness describe the forest and its effect on the human psyche. Apprehensions regarding the unknown path, both literal and metaphoric, abound, and light imagery figures prominently in a frontier literature of darkness.

Sketch of a typical Indiana frontier cabin swallowed up in forest.

Whether it was the beauty of woods standing "up to the ankles in white mist"[2] or the "sombre, limitless wall of trees that seemed to close in with smothering relentlessness about the lonely cabin,"[3] trees were the one common element, the most visible and unrelenting reality of the frontier Indiana experience. And trees became the most constant image of the frontier experience in the state's literature, from Indiana's earliest novel to some of its most recent.

In the 1967 novel *Leafy Rivers*, Indiana author Jessamyn West writes with wry humor about the westward movement.

> We looked on our trip, at the start, like a park stroll. Outdoors, to be sure, but a good time of the year and under the shelter of trees. Under the shelter of trees! That tells the story. We'd as well have made the journey underground, crawled the whole distance through a culvert. Except for one thing. The trees being alive you had a different feeling for them than you had for the dirt of a cave,

or the timber or stone of a culvert. They're alive, and, like anything live, they had feelings. They could be won over. Or so we hoped.

Shortly thereafter, the narrator amends, "but they're like an animal, too. They take advantage of you if you're afraid."[4]

This paradox of the frontier experience is a common motif in American literature. The very aspects of wilderness that appealed to the pioneer spirit in man were the ones man strove to correct. Vastness begged to be contained and filled. Silence and solitude to be enlivened. Darkness to be lit. Wildness to be tamed. When nature resisted, it was unfailingly characterized as savage, cruel, and repellent, and thereby deserving of its fate.

At the same time the natural world was depicted as being helpless before the advance of civilization. In countless novels of the early Indiana frontier, trees become the metaphor for all of nature in distress. In West's *Leafy Rivers*, once a habitation has been wrested from the wilderness the battle for territory has really only just begun and the struggle assumes an even more personal dimension.

> The Lucey front yard was a sorry sight. It was packed dirt without a bush or tree on it. This was exactly what Elizabeth Lucey wanted. She had seen, in her trip through the woods from Carolina to Ohio, enough trees to last her a lifetime. A vine she could tolerate, but nothing, not even a lilac bush or peony, with power of its own to lift itself up, cast a shadow, and block the way. One thing she had left in her yard—a big hickory stump, waist-high, stripped of its bark. Mrs. Lucey treated this as furniture. She scrubbed the top of it, she stretched cloths for bleaching across it, she stacked it with milk pans to sun.
>
> The stump was bare this afternoon, and Chancellor thought it looked, in the clear slanting light, white and menacing, like the one mean tooth left in an empty mouth. Or a tombstone. Though what it actually was, he supposed, was a skeleton; or at least the stump of one. Mrs. Lucey kept it there as a message for the rest of the forest: Stay

away from my door, if you don't want this to happen to you.[5]

West depicts the Lucey yard as the graveyard of the forest, the last tooth in a landscape that has lost its bite.

In *Freckles*, Gene Stratton-Porter carries the domestication of trees a step farther. "Of the thousands who saw their faces reflected on the polished surfaces of that furniture and found comfort in its use, few there were to whom it suggested mighty forests and trackless swamps, and the man, big of soul and body, who cut his way through them, and with the eye of experience doomed the proud trees that were now entering the homes of civilization for service."[6] Similarly, in *The Cubical City*, by Janet Flanner, a young woman is unaware that her efforts to pastoralize her New York apartment represent a subconscious nostalgia for the small, green Indiana town she has left behind.

> What had once been trees from open spaces were long since turned to beams, gilded and carved, before they had been set up in her rooms and the only visible leaves and flowers were those flattened by her feet on the garden of her rug. Yet in the midst of these falsified forests, these buds from the loom, this air where clouds were stale perfume and a strong lamp was the sun, she sat as if she were suitably settled in some verdant free field. A renter of hired space in New York, still she seemed to be a native of natural seasons whose cosmic burgeoning she carried on in town, thriving like a big boned blond sapling whose sap and shifting leaves made seasons under a roof.[7]

In this artificial environment even "the flowers on the table had been forced and made to blossom and swell in the domiciled heat."[8]

So boundless and daunting was the forest that it had seemed inexhaustible. Certainly "economy did not enter into the question," Charles Major wrote in *A Forest Hearth: A Romance of Indiana in the Thirties*, "for wood was nature's chief weapon against her enemies, the settlers; and the question was not how to save, but how to burn it."[9]

As the vast native forest disappeared, many Indiana novelists recognized the importance of cataloging and celebrating the variety and abundance of trees that filled it. "There are two different kinds of timber land in this county," Kate Milner Rabb wrote in *A Tour through Indiana in 1840*. "The flats, as we denominate them, are covered with large and tall timber, white oak, beech, gum, soft maple, burr oak, hickory, and some other varieties, with a thick undergrowth in many sections, interwoven with grapevines. The second is the rolling land, where grow profusely the white oak, the black oak, the beech, the sugar tree, the linden, the ash, the black walnut, the white walnut, the cherry and the poplar, with an undergrowth, on the rich bottoms, of pawpaw and an occasional large sassafras. On the bottom lands along the streams, sycamore, hackberry, elm and buckeye flourish."[10]

In *Jack Shelby: A Story of the Indiana Backwoods*, George C. Eggleston recalls that "here and there in the beechwoods, there stood clumps of hickory, or ash, or oak, or walnut, and at certain points there were great groves of sugar maples, or 'sugar trees' as they were called in Southern Indiana . . . almost as black as ink, because every spring their over-abundant sap, or 'sugar water' oozed out and dried on the bark to the color of ink."[11]

Jessamyn West in *The Massacre at Fall Creek* lists "maples, sycamores, beeches, oaks, walnuts . . . there had once been a stand of ash, the settler's most valued tree." This inventory is taken by characters en route to a hanging, where the trees are essential to the mode of execution. "When they came through the woods to where the stand of ash had been cut, the gibbet was visible.

"Wonder what trees think, being put to that use?" Charlie asks, to which his companion responds, "Don't say things like that to anybody else, Charlie."[12]

Speculation about nature was rich with dramatic potential for authors of Indiana fiction. In much of Indiana literature nature evolves from an impersonal force to a character in its own right, most notably through the anthropomorphizing of trees by the human characters in the books. In novel after novel, trees laugh, whisper, cry, shriek, experience pain as well as joy, conspire, observe, and judge.

In a Civil War novel, *The Test of Loyalty*, by James M. Hiatt, the trees are again witnesses to an execution. "The heavens are draped in black, and the massive green heads of the forest giants seem bowed in the spirit of mourning, while a heavy breeze is playing a melancholy requiem among their drooping boughs."[13] And in George Barr McCutcheon's *Kindling and Ashes*, trees and frontier justice are again inextricably bound when Old Benjamin chops down the "family tree" from which his father had, before Benjamin was born, been hanged for stealing a horse. "It was an oak tree," Old Benjamin recalls.[14]

From their natural vantage point of looking down upon humankind, trees often appear as judges to be feared, or at the very least as elders to be respected, even venerated, though this regard seldom extended to the point of sparing them. "They felt themselves absorbing into something deep and still and pro-foundly comforting. Something came out of the woods, and flowed over them and through them, and they just sat there and let themselves dissolve. . . . The trees looked down at them, talk-ing confidentially," writes Marthedith Furnas in *A Serpent's Tooth*.[15]

In *A Girl of the Limberlost* by Gene Stratton-Porter, perhaps Indiana's foremost wielder of anthropomorphic license, the hero-ine Elnora captivates her would-be suitor with her vivid imagina-tion. "You know all trees whisper and talk during the summer, but there are two that have so much to say they keep on the whole winter, when the others are silent. The beeches and oaks so love to talk, they cling to their dead, dry leaves. In the winter the winds are stiffest and blow most, so these trees whisper, chatter, sob, laugh, and at times roar until the sound is deafening. They never cease until new leaves come out in the spring to push off the old ones. I love to stand beneath them with my ear to the great trunks, interpreting what they say to fit my moods. The beeches branch low, and their leaves are small so they only know common earthly things; but the oaks run straight above almost all other trees before they branch, their arms are mighty, their leaves large. They meet the winds that travel around the globe, and from them learn the big things."[16]

Trees talk to people. Sometimes people talk to trees. In the 1993 novel *The True Life Story of Isobel Roundtree*, by Kathleen Wallace King, the child Isobel, sensing impending destruction of the woods by local developers, flees to her grandfather's woods. "Out in the woods I talked to the trees. It was the only way I could calm down, be peaceful. I sang to the trees. Talking to the trees gave me a kind of deep-down power. I could feel it running into me where I touched their tough bark. I would lean up against them and smell the sap deep inside—tree blood.

"My grandpa, who died when his heart exploded while he was shoveling snow, never had the trees cut down to plant more land. My grandpa knew about trees."[17]

Even a cutting-edge sci-fi novel, *Alternities*, which takes as its theme a parallel universe, back and forth to which the protagonist travels through a gate in the Scottish Rite Cathedral in Indianapolis, includes a scene in humble old Yellowwood Forest in southern Indiana. "I call it the grandmother tree . . . it's a white oak, like most of these. They can live seven hundred years . . . standing here and watching the world. . . . It was already old when this land belonged to the Algonkin and the Iroquois . . . when the whole state was oak-hickory forest as far as you could see, before the French started cutting trees to build their forts and their fires. Do you see how the younger trees seem to give it room, out of respect? They're her children and grandchildren."[18] In this 1988 novel by Michael P. Kube-McDowell, the forest serves as a sanctuary in the midst of sinister high-tech plotting and shenanigans.

The clearing and cultivation of the vast Indiana Territory represented to some authors the final victory and to other authors rapacious plunder. Authors inclined to the latter point of view went to some lengths to imbue the doomed trees with human, and thereby sympathetic, emotions. Several authors described the process of deadening to future audiences. In *Thad Perkins: A Story of Early Indiana*, Frank A. Myers explains that "the timber had been girdled with an ax the winter before, and left standing for the ravages of time to finish the work of clearing the ground. These dead timber wastes were, in the parlance of the times, called deadenings."[19]

Indiana writer James Baldwin in his fictionalized autobiography, *In My Youth*, likewise describes " 'the new deadenin,' where hundreds of leafless trees stand in mute agony, lifting their gaunt arms toward heaven as though dumbly protesting against the cruelty of the man who has girdled their trunks and doomed them to a lingering death. And finally, beyond this landscape of fields, pastureland, bottom and deadening, rises the forest primeval, 'the big woods,' a region of mystery, stretching away and away to the very rim of the sky, the edge of the world."[20] A seemingly inexhaustible resource.

Deadening actually preceded the white man, as George C. Eggleston notes in *Jack Shelby*. "They didn't cut the trees down, but they girdled them just as white men do nowadays in what we call a 'deadening.' That is to say they cut through the bark in a ring around the lower part of the tree, so that the sap could not flow, and the trees must die."[21]

Die they did, by the hundreds of thousands, as the sound of the ax reverberated in the frontier forest and the "startled echoes from the 'tall timber' of the dark dens, were telling each other that the centuries of a wood-monarch were numbered!"[22] In this and numerous other passages of *The New Purchase; or, Seven and a Half Years in the Far West*, Baynard Rush Hall, Indiana's earliest novelist, laments the desecration in melodramatic prose intended to stir the reader's conscience. "Alas! oh! noble tree, you tremble! Ah! it is not the deep and accustomed thunder of the heavens, that shakes you now!—no mighty quaking of the earth! . . . Hark!—the mighty heart is breaking!"[23]

After the girdling came the felling of the trees and "the oak, which had answered ax strokes with dull defiance at first, had lifted its bass notes to a piping treble as the blades on the opposite sides approached its heart; and before the final citadel was taken, the great tree shivered, then slowly turned, and surrendering, swept with a mighty sound of branches rushing through the air, of timber rending, and a sudden impact on the stubborn ground."[24]

LeRoy Armstrong, the author of the above passage from *The Outlaws: A Story of the Building of the West*, called the process "preparing [the] monarch of the forest for his funeral pyre"[25] because hard upon the heels of the deadenings followed wholesale burning of timber that could not be used in building or heating a cabin. Hall describes this stage of destruction as vividly as he did the former. "Far and wide the forest was grandly illuminated; and in returning home I often looked back and saw the noble trees at the pyres, tossing their mighty arms and bowing their spreading tops for mercy and succour—ay! like beings sending forth cries of agony unheard in that fiery chaos!"[26]

Myers was moved by these images of fire and agony in *Thad Perkins*. "In the clearing the blue smoke, seen in the red fire-light of the burning log heaps, curled upward like a thing struggling in pain, and the odor of burning wood was wafted to the lad's keen olfactories. He sniffed it like a joy . . . the crackling, snapping sound of the brush he tossed into the lurid flames reminded him of the spiteful snarls of hateful little wood sprites of the night . . . what trembling tongues of flame lit up the mighty scene like a section of the infernal regions transferred to earth!"[27]

The great forest was ripe for association with all manner of spiritual and scriptural imagery. Even the most commonplace sensory images take on an almost supernatural aura in the loneliness, silence, and isolation of the Indiana wilderness. Literary historians have charted the course of spiritual wilderness imagery from such diverse sources as Dante and Hebrew scripture, as Simon Schama points out in *Landscape and Memory*. "The dark wood" was "a place where one lost one's way." Schama contends that "the indeterminate, boundless forest . . . was Europe's version of the Hebraic desert wilderness . . . a place where the faith of the true believer would be put to the severest tests."[28] Leonard Lutwack suggests that the Puritans simply "adapted Christian stereotypes of the dark wood and barren desert to American geography," and that this "milder adaptation . . . saw the American wilderness as a testing ground in which to build strong moral character."[29] In other words, to build the ideal of the courageous frontiersman, the noble pioneer, the quintessential American.

Baldwin makes the direct association in *In My Youth* when he compares his early Indiana home with "perhaps the wilderness wherein the Israelites wandered with Moses."[30] In Jessamyn West's beloved *The Friendly Persuasion*, a poignant scene unfolds at a most opportune moment when a disillusioned Quaker farm family unearths a piece of scripture torn from an ancestor's Old Testament. "Call thy mother. . . . Call the boys," the patriarch of the family shouts. "This is no happen-chance. This is something buried a purpose for our later having. Something set in the earth with foresight."[31] The buried passage of scripture read, "And the Lord brought us forth out of Egypt with a mighty hand . . . and with an outstretched arm and with great terribleness and with signs and with wonders. And he hath brought us into this place and hath given us this land, even a land that floweth with milk and honey."[32]

The characters in Nancy N. Baxter's *The Movers: A Saga of the Scotch-Irish* see "the mark of the beast . . . on all these forests, along with the promise of God. . . . The forest had the power to turn them, all of them out here, into beasts or gods. It depended. On what? On what you let the forest do to you."[33]

Hebrew symbolism yielded to Christian imagery, in the form of the circuit rider, in many Indiana novels. Edward Eggleston paid especial attention to the profession, undoubtedly due to his early personal experience as a Methodist circuit rider. In the novel that bears the very title, he refers to that "favorite oratory of the early Methodist preacher, the forest."[34] And in another novel, *The Graysons*, Eggleston's vivid depictions of camp meetings make it clear why the perils of the forest could be so readily manipulated for evangelistic purposes. "The bonfires on the platforms illuminated the circle of white tents, which stood out against the wall of deep blackness in the forest behind; the light mounted a hundred feet and more through the thick branches of lofty beech and maple trees, and was reflected from the under side of leaves quivering in the breeze. The boughs and foliage, illuminated from below, had an unreal and unworldly aspect. No imagery of the preacher could make the threatened outer darkness of the lost so weird to the imagination as this scene, in which the company of simple-minded people found themselves in the presence of a savage Nature, and in a sphere of light bounded on every hand by a blackness as of darkness primeval."[35]

The contrasts between the light of the meeting and the dark of the forest, "the region of outer blackness, quite beyond the reach of any illumination from platform bonfires or pulpit eloquence,"[36] is stark and anything but subtle, and in fact the imagery is sometimes slightly suggestive of pagan rituals rather than of Christian worship. Indiana authors frequently played with the social and entertainment value of camp meetings in the wilderness where the pious and the merely curious took advantage of an opportunity to carouse and cavort with impunity under the guise of spiritual transport. Hall attributed this phenomenon to a landscape-induced, as well as culturally induced, hysteria. "To the imaginative, there is very much to bewitch in the poetry and romance of a Western camp-meeting—the wildness, the gloom, the grandeur of our forests . . . how like a spirit world, a residence of ransomed ones! The very tents, too!—formed like booths at the feast of tabernacles . . . a community having all things common, dead to the world, just ready to enter heaven!"[37]

In *Dionis of the White Veil*, by Indiana author Caroline Brown, characters are literally being prepared to enter heaven. This novel, set in virgin wilderness just being penetrated by the Jesuits, suggests the primitive in its depiction of the first mass offered at the sight of a new mission. "Thus the Druids once may have served their gods, in the midst of trees dripping dew like holy water; . . . with haze spread abroad, blue and sweet as incense, from the fume of Autumn's decay; with an arched roof above them loftier than any of man's constructing . . . with aisles stretched behind them through the forest, longer and dimmer than those in the vastness of Saint Peter's, with the golden light of the newly risen sun illuminating all, brighter than a thousand candles."[38] It is particularly appropriate that the author points out that the forest is vaster than any human construction and the light of the sun brighter than mere man-made candles. Just as the priest is reciting the Kyrie Eleison, the presumed friendly Indians in attendance massacre the party, "bespattering the wilderness altar with a blood-offering."[39] It is a graphic triumph, however temporary, of the indigenous and primitive.

The perils of the frontier were numerous and are familiar to readers of Indiana history. Caroline Brown filled her novels with "sudden floods, treacherous under currents, hidden sand-bars, savage beasts and venomous reptiles; worse than all, the haunting, deadly savage!"[40] And Jessamyn West made effective use of "swamps, ague, broken axles, meal turned bad, fords washed out, unmarked crossings, torrential downpours. And the forest so thick them days it was like traveling in a cave."[41]

The domestication or destruction of native flora and fauna, the increasing permanence of human habitation, the demise of an agricultural economy to make way for an industrial economy, and of a rural culture to make way for an urban culture, all have found expression in Indiana literature. In *The Role of Place in Literature*, Lutwack notes that "a kind of moral geography springs from man's ability to adapt himself to hostile environments."[42] It would seem that the same geography springs from man's ability to adapt the environment to his own purposes, which is the story of the American frontier and, in some aspect, of all midwestern literature.

CHAPTER TWO

Pride and Protest

Local Color and the Early Realists

When what could be called the novel first made its appearance in the raw Indiana Territory it was so immature and so shaped by the pioneer experience that it essentially appeared as thinly disguised autobiography. Two such efforts, both exercises in personal protest, appeared at approximately the same time: Baynard Rush Hall's *The New Purchase; or, Seven and a Half Years in the Far West* and Eunice Beecher's *From Dawn to Daylight; or, the Simple Story of a Western Home*.

Hall slightly preceded Beecher, in experience of the Indiana frontier and in publication, but they were contemporaries in that their "novels" tend to corroborate contested aspects of their respective experiences. They certainly shared in the public outcries and unpopularity that greeted the publication of their books. The books were written under pseudonyms, Robert Carlton, Esq., in the case of Hall, and "a minister's wife" in the case of Beecher; however, their identities were well known within their own communities.

The New Purchase was part travel narrative, both challenging and championing the frontier experience. Hall was a Philadelphian and a graduate of Union College and Princeton Theological Seminary. He had a genuine fascination with the West, and he and his wife came to what was then called "the new purchase" around 1821, only in part because Hall had his eye on a position at the newly established Indiana State Seminary in Bloomington. Hall was hired in 1823 and served as the entire faculty until, in his fourth year, John Hopkins Harney joined the faculty. Shortly thereafter, in 1828, the institution became the

Indiana College, and Andrew Wylie became its first president in 1829.

The contemporary reader can well imagine what must have been Hall's culture shock upon moving to this raw wilderness, recently obtained by treaty from the Indians. Bloomington was three years old at the time of Hall's arrival and could claim fewer than three hundred inhabitants, none of them particularly amenable to higher education. Arthur W. Shumaker makes note in *A History of Indiana Literature* of Hall's first group of scholars as "ten backwoods boys . . . who came to class coatless and shoeless."[1] Hall repeatedly found himself caught between a state legislature that had mandated the instruction of Latin, Greek, and mathematics, and local politicians and citizenry who, if they had any use for the college at all, valued more practical subjects such as "book-keepin' and surveyin'."[2] While serious disagreements with President Wylie and almost indecipherable academic politics caused Harney to be dismissed and led Hall to resign in 1831 and return East, Hall never acclimated to his new surroundings.

Hall and his wife had set out from Philadelphia full of pioneer zeal, traveling by stagecoach to Pittsburgh and then down the Ohio River to Louisville. "Oh!" Hall wrote in his exuberance, "the change from dark, damp, stifling pent holes of alleys and courts, where filth exhales its stench without the sun!—to walk abroad, run, leap, ride, hunt and shout, amid the unwrought, unsubdued, boundless world of primitive forest, flood, and prairie!" Hall wanted "to see the world as the Omnipotent made it and the deluge left it! . . . the Indian . . . in the drapery of untouched forests and midst the fragrance of the ungardened, many coloured, ever-varied flowers!"[3]

But very quickly the Halls and their counterparts in the narrative were "buried in the darkness of the forest."[4] Once they had left the Ohio they were ill-prepared for the true nature of the southern Indiana wilderness with its "deafening clangour of innumerable rude frogs in the mires and on the trees . . . the whirl and hum and buzz of strange, savage insects and reptiles, and of winged and unwinged bugs [that] began and increased and grew still louder; and vapours [that] damp, chilly and foetid ascended and came down."[5] Hall quickly repented of his lust for adventure. "However romantic such a wild may be in print," he wrote, "my thoughts in the wilderness itself, were all concentrated on one object—the path. And long what seemed the path, dim always and sometimes obliterated, as it led far away into the gloom of impervious shades . . . this trace occupied all my meditations and excited my intensest watchings and kept me asking in a mental and often an audible voice,—'I *do* wonder, if this *is* the way?' To which, as nobody replied, I would answer myself—'Well, I guess it *must* be—if this is not, I'm sure I don't see any *other*!' "[6]

Mrs. Carlton, the fictional Mrs. Hall, who had been "persuaded to exchange the tasteless and crowded solitude of Philadelphia for the entrancing and real loneliness of the wilds, and the promenade of dead brick for the living carpet of the natural meadow,"[7] was given less to existential ruminating, or to complaint, though she occasionally voiced tentative reservations. "Who *could* have dreamed, my dear . . . these forests so picturesque when seen from the Ohio, concealed such roads?"[8]

The new arrivals fared no better when they reached their destination. "We stood in the edge of the wilderness," Hall wrote of the tiny new campus, "late the lurking place of the Indian, and yet concealing the bear, the wolf, the panther."[9] Even supposedly domesticated animals rivaled the beasts of the forest as when Hall complains of " 'the neighbors' hogs', so wild and fierce, that when pork-time arrives, they must be hunted and shot, like other independent beasts."[10]

In the novel the town of Woodville stood for Bloomington. Hall commented that the town was "large, however, for its age, and dirty as an undisciplined, neglected urchin of the same years, and rough as a motherless cub."[11] When the Carltons arrived in their new community they were shocked by the condition of the "two unfinished brick buildings, destined for the use of the future University. . . . The smaller house was crammed with somebody's hay and flax; while the larger was pouring forth a flock of sheep."[12]

Similarly the Carltons were unprepared for what Hall referred to as "Hoosiers and all other wild men."[13] While dining with their hosts in one cabin the Carltons recognized "in the midst of other good things, and full of milk, the republican bowl that a few moments before had enacted the part of wash-basin."[14]

In the novel the Carltons quickly learn the local norms of acceptably democratic behavior. Mrs. Carlton, in particular, is deemed to be too proud by virtue of her standards of cleanliness and modesty. She is faulted for not wearing the coarsely woven caps that all local wives wore, not only as a sign of their marital status, but also " 'to save slicking up every day, and to hide dirt!' "[15] Similarly, when as an overnight guest in a stranger's cabin she puts up a makeshift partition before undressing and retiring, her behavior is deemed to be " 'powerful proud doings of stuck-up folks.' "[16] If the local inhabitants found the Carltons to be a bit aristocratic during their tenure in Bloomington, they found them to be intolerably so after their departure and the publication of *The New Purchase*.

Hall's greatest contribution to Indiana literature is in his detailed and probably faithful depictions of pioneer life in southern Indiana. In his book he vividly recorded events such as cabin raisings, camp meetings, shivarees, barbeques, and "electioneering." He also captured local dialect and the attitudes of the Hoosier pioneers, including preachers who would boast " 'I never rub'd my back agin a collige, nor git no sheepskin, and allow the Apostuls didn't nithur.' "[17]

Despite the hardships of travel—"mudholes, quicksands, quagmires, marshes, high waters"[18]—Hall had an intense desire to see as much of Indiana as he could and to record his experiences, both positive and negative. He took every opportunity to make long journeys on horseback, usually on business for either the Presbyterian church or the college. While he could not say enough about the poor conditions of the roads, a common lament of all early travel writers, he found much to delight him. "Away we splashed," he wrote, "kicking up . . . a . . . shower of aqueous particles, and many a smart sprinkle of mud, that rattled like hail on the leaves above, and the backs and shoulders below." It was, he lamented, "dirt-coloured rain."[19] In almost the same breath he would exude, "shall I tell how, in crossing a prairie, we saw, oh! I don't know how many deer!—nor how we started up prairie fowls, hens and roosters . . . yes, and saw prairie wolves too, a cantering from us over the plain!"[20] Of the prairies between Crawfordsville and Lafayette, Hall wrote that an "awe is felt at the grandeur of the wild plains . . . picturesque meadows, fringed with thickets intervening, and separating the primitive pasturages as in the golden age! The green and flowery meads seemed made for flocks and herds: and imagination easily created, under the shade of trees, shepherds and shepherdesses, with crooks and sylvan reeds! It heard the sound of pipes!"[21]

It is clear that Hall nursed a love/hate relationship with Indiana. As time passed Hall arrived at something close to fondness for the eccentricities of his adopted state and its inhabitants. He found great humor in the propensity of Americans, in general, and of Hoosiers, in particular, to swap stories and spin yarns in which they exaggerated the size and magnificence of everything native. "And this is a fair chance to say a word about the enormous *circumambitudialitariness* of many western trees," he quipped in *The New Purchase*. "It is common to find such from six to seven feet in diameter; and we have more than once sat on stumps and measured across three lengths of my cane, nearly ten feet; and found, on counting the concentric circles, that these monsters must have been from seven to eight hundred years old—an age greater than Noah's, and almost as venerable as that of Methusaleh! Shall we feel no sublimity in walking amid and around such ancients?"[22]

The height, circumference, and age of trees was an endless source not only of fascination but also of native pride. In part, the impulse to brag about trees was an infant culture's attempt to claim a legitimate measure of antiquity. "If history is short in America," Leonard Lutwack noted in *The Role of Place in Literature*, "geologic time may be invoked to fill it out to respectable mythic proportion."[23] In raising up Indiana's "forest dark and venerable with the growth of many centuries,"[24] Hall had his finger on the pulse of the nation and his adopted region. "And dare finical European tourists say we have no antiquity! Poor souls!—poor souls!—our trees were fit for navies, long years before their old things existed! Ay, when their oldest castles and cities were unwrought rock and unburnt clay! Our trees belong to the era of Egyptian architecture—they are coeval with the pyramids!"[25] Compared to this "great wooden country,"[26] the modest forests of Europe paled.

In addition to genuine awe respecting the size, scope, and antiquity of the great forest that virtually covered the early Indiana Territory, Hall was also making sport of the tendency in travel accounts to exaggerate the wonders to be encountered in the West, as in this clearly overdrawn depiction from the novel: "Near the junction of the White River of Indiana and the Wabash, stands a sycamore fully ninety feet in circumference! Within its hollow can be stabled a dozen horses."[27]

If Hall's "circumambitudialitariness" was a good-natured joke at the expense of his frontier neighbors, the size of American trees did awe and inspire early travelers and "most . . . who descended the Ohio River by flatboat managed at some point along the way to measure a giant tree,"[28] according to John A. Jakle in *Images of the Ohio Valley: A Historical Geography of Travel, 1740 to 1860.* Indeed, early photographs attest to this pastime. A popular unit of measure was the number of men required to encircle a tree, touching hand to hand. And it was not an exaggeration according to Jakle that "many of the giant sycamores were hollow and could accommodate a man on horseback,"[29] if not stable a dozen horses. Regardless, Hall could not resist the temptation to heckle in homespun vernacular. "All things out there are big: if two things of the same name are to be distinguished, one is called big, and the other powerful big."[30]

Hall left Bloomington in 1831 greatly disillusioned and marked, both positively and negatively, by his sojourn in Indiana. During his tenure at the state college, which would become Indiana University in 1838, Hall's income had been so paltry that he supplemented it by serving as pastor of the Presbyterian church of Bloomington; his salary, Shumaker notes, "being paid in items of trade."[31] Hall's book was published more than a decade after his resignation, but its publication caused an uproar in the town of Bloomington and scandal within the university itself.

Eunice Beecher about the time her unpopular book was suppressed in Indianapolis.

Hall's circumstances were so similar to those experienced by Eunice Beecher, the long-suffering wife of Henry Ward Beecher, that even if her short novel, *From Dawn to Daylight*, published in 1859, does not merit the serious consideration that his lengthy narrative does, it still stands as an excellent resource for exploring the Indiana pioneer experience.

Eunice's little book contains no elements of a travel account and no attempts to impress, educate, or entice the folks back home. Her book is pure protest, though she probably intended it as a vindication of her experiences and reputation.

There may have been unhappier frontier wives than Eunice Beecher, but not many of them would have been able or inclined to write about their experiences. Born in 1812 to an established Massachusetts family, Eunice White Bullard was a schoolteacher when she met and married Henry Ward Beecher. Their honeymoon in 1837 was actually their passage to Lawrenceburg, Indiana,

Eunice Beecher as a young frontier mother, before her sojourn in Indiana had taken its toll on her face or her temperament.

where Henry had landed his first pastorate. Although Eunice was seriously ill during most of their trip west, Henry, ever ambitious, took every opportunity to greet congregations and preach along the way, thereby cultivating contacts and establishing his reputation in communities throughout the East and Middle West.

Eunice had the best of intentions when setting out with her charismatic young husband into the new missionary field. But the romantic appeal of the western frontier soon faded into bitter disillusionment in much the same way that it had for Hall and his wife. Eunice despaired of her isolation and the primitive sensibilities of her neighbors. She deplored the muddy, rutted roads and village streets where pigs and sheep were free to roam. New to the West, she was also new to marriage, to motherhood, and to the role of minister's wife, a particularly thankless and impoverished position in the West. Eunice had had expectations, based upon the highly regarded position of clergy in the East, of enjoying a certain level of status and privilege. Early in the novel, Mary Leighton, the fictional Eunice, assures her father by letter that "I'm the *minister's wife* now, and you'll see how grave I shall be . . . I haven't become so accustomed to my honors as to feel quite sure that I shall wear them with proper dignity."[32]

Eunice quickly realized that a minister's life was anything but dignified in the West, where pioneers were suspicious of an educated clergy and where a minister's salary was regarded, by many, as charity. She deeply resented being on the receiving end of donations of food, secondhand clothing, and discarded household items. "There was wealth in abundance among their new people," Mary Leighton lamented. "The money wasted on parties and frivolous amusements every few weeks, would have comfortably supported their pastor's family a year, and given his wife an opportunity to rest and regain her strength."[33]

Regaining her strength was a major concern. Eunice had been burdened with ill health since she had arrived in Indiana, but it became especially problematic when the Beechers moved to Indianapolis, a city whose climate and terrain was particularly suited to "ague." More than the mud and mosquitoes, more than deprivation, loneliness, and "labor beyond the strength,"[34] it was probably the relentless cycle of pregnancy, childbirth, and grief that weakened Eunice's constitution. Eunice delivered five of her children in Indiana, and she buried two of them there. Meanwhile Henry was busy rising to a level of prominence in everything from local politics and education to the volunteer fire department. He traveled extensively and enjoyed a national reputation while Eunice stayed at home and suffered the indignities peculiar to a minister's wife. "The minister's wife must be out among the people, or they will find fault. She must head the Sewing Society and Maternal Association, and preside at the Female Prayer Meeting, be 'at home' to calls, at all hours of the day, and of the most unmerciful length, from the very ones, perhaps, who will go away and wonder that Mrs. _____'s floors were not cleaner."[35]

It is significant that in biographies of Henry, Eunice merits only cursory mention. It is instructive, as well, that the author credit for *From Dawn to Daylight* reads "by a minister's wife" as late as 1859. Nowhere does Eunice Beecher's name appear in the text. Eunice wrote in her preface, "Some years since, I prepared the following sketch of the life of a dear friend, with whose history I had been familiar."[36] This statement, combined with the book's curious credit, fueled rumors that Eunice was attempting to hide her identity, but it probably had more to do with gender. Such expressions were not uncommon in an age when women seldom wrote, and when those who did frequently used male pseudonyms or were referred to simply as Mrs. _____. Furthermore, if Eunice's motive in writing *From Dawn to Daylight* had indeed been "personal protest"[37] as Arthur Shumaker suggests, then anonymity would scarcely have been her objective. In fact, Eunice may have been commenting quite eloquently on her condition by her choice of credits.

The modern reader is, after all, not convinced that protest was Mrs. Beecher's only objective. Although an early column in the *Indianapolis Times* called the story "a dreary affair" penned with the "acid bite of a disappointed woman,"[38] and another columnist in the *Indianapolis News* proclaimed that "the book itself possessed no literary merit and had no excuse for being"[39] other than spite, the fact remains that the only thing that distinguished Eunice Beecher as a person was her novel.

From Dawn to Daylight is not without literary merit. Eunice was an educated woman, and even her personal letters are written with a style, charm, and clarity that are indisputable. Her prose is at times almost luminous, as in the novel when she captures perfectly an oppressive summer afternoon in Indiana. "It is a still, sultry August day—a 'fever breeder,' as the doctor said this morning. Little Susie has fallen asleep on the settee. The clock ticks sadly on the mantel, the flies crawl lazily over the window, with a ceaseless buzz, that makes me shiver. The shadows of the beautiful locust-trees look ghostly, as they fall athwart the grass, or flicker noiselessly in the sunlight, on the floor. How painfully still it is!"[40]

A dispassionate reading of *From Dawn to Daylight* reveals a steady evolution in Mary's feelings toward Norton, which stood for

Indianapolis, and her husband's parishioners. The first part of the story is told in the form of letters from Mary to her mother in which she vents her frustration in references to such things as mud and pigs, "these two articles, the staple commodity of this far-famed region,"[41] and "pale, sallow, unhealthy-looking people."[42] But such petulant remarks appear early in the novel and by a third of the way through the book, Eunice has tempered her presentation considerably. "The city . . . presents quite a thriving appearance, being very prettily laid out, with a number of fine buildings. Excepting in the main business streets, the houses are not so *huddled* together, after the manner of our eastern cities; but each has a fine back and front yard, and the streets are broad, with shade-trees on either side. On the whole, when seen on a fair, sunlighted day, it is rather attractive at first sight."[43]

In fact, far from being an unflattering portrait of Indianapolis, *From Dawn to Daylight* is more a revelation of a clergyman's lot than an indictment of a particular congregation or community. What made *From Dawn to Daylight* infamous had more to do with Indianapolis recognizing itself and reading between the lines than with actual malice.

But infamous it was. The book caused such a sensation that it was effectively banned by public sentiment in Indianapolis. The wounds were so deep that the bitterness lingered for decades. *From Dawn to Daylight* was not published until twelve years after the Beechers left Indiana, and some thirty years later Eunice was still talking about Indianapolis. And Indianapolis was still talking about her.

That the wife of Henry Ward Beecher could have effected such a whirlwind of controversy may be more to her credit than discredit. The plight of the pioneer woman was a frequent theme in the short fiction of another early Indiana author who had her own ax to grind with respect to the conventions of marriage and the constraints of western society. Mary Hartwell Catherwood was born the year the Beechers left Indianapolis, and Indiana was a much different place by the time she began her literary career. The fact that a woman could pursue a literary career at all was the least of it.

Catherwood was born in Ohio and lived in Illinois, New York State, and then Cincinnati before marrying in 1877 and moving to Howard County, Indiana. Like Eunice Beecher, Catherwood had been a schoolteacher, though unlike Eunice she had literary aspirations at an early age, publishing her first stories and poems at the age of sixteen. Catherwood's life was one of many "firsts." Fred Lewis Pattee in *A History of American Literature since 1870* claimed that Catherwood was "the first woman of any prominence in American literary ranks to acquire a college education,"[44] and it was significant to him that she was graduated from Granville Female Seminary in Ohio rather than from an eastern institution. Pattee further claimed that Catherwood was "the first woman novelist of the period to be born west of the Alleghenies."[45] In R. E. Banta's *Indiana Authors and Their Books, 1816–1916*, Robert Price, in his essay about Catherwood, refers to her as "the pioneer woman writer of the Middle West."[46] Though Arthur Shumaker quibbles with certain of these assertions, he confirms that "no serious student of American literature—to say nothing of Indiana literature—from the Civil War to the turn of the century can afford to overlook her work."[47]

Prior to coming to Indiana Catherwood's fiction and poetry had been "mediocre . . . and . . . perfunctorily romantic,"[48] according to Shumaker. Ironically, it was her life in the tiny town of Oakford, Indiana (formerly Fairfield), that not only provided the material for her most vivid local-color fiction, but also launched her on a brief career as one of the nation's early critical realists, winning her the regard of such a notable as William Dean Howells.

The Catherwoods as newlyweds lived over the train station in Oakford and, according to Shumaker, it was here that Mrs. Catherwood began reporting what she saw to be the "ugliness and narrowness of mind found in rural life and in small towns."[49] In fact, it was from the grim perspective of frontier Indiana that the author began to write disparagingly of former climes, such as in the novel *Craque-O'-Doom*, which was written in Indianapolis, but which tells the story of her unhappy childhood in Hebron, Ohio. While living in Indiana she wrote several unflattering short stories set in Ohio and Illinois, though the various model communities are disguised. Interestingly enough, however, several of her Indiana stories are set in Oakford, thinly disguised by the use of its former name. Indeed, one is called "The Fairfield Poet," and another, "Mallston's Youngest," which appeared in *Lippincott's Magazine* in August 1880, is set in Fairfield by name, as well. Compounding this dubious honor is the fact that the Indiana stories have the least attractive characters of any of Catherwood's short fiction.

Two Indiana stories were included in 1899 in the collection *The Queen of the Swamp, and Other Plain Americans*. By this time Catherwood had repented of her early realism and was on her way to becoming an outspoken advocate of romanticism in literature, a curious return to former estates, inspired in large part by her friendship with James Whitcomb Riley and exposure to his wholesome, sentimental portrayals of rural and small-town charms. In a very brief author's note that prefaced the collection Catherwood seems to be apologizing for its harsh tone by assuring the reader that "some of these stories were written more than a dozen years ago." She hastens to add that "many of them embody phases of American life which have entirely passed away, or are yet to be found in secluded spots like eddies along the margin of the nation's progress."[50] By this time Catherwood had already published her tremendously popular *The Romance of Dollard* and had carried on a well-publicized feud in print with Hamlin Garland regarding the merits of realism, Catherwood criticizing realism and minimizing its long-term importance to American literature.

Nevertheless, regarding her short fiction, Catherwood herself could not resist the impulse to point out "their honest preservation of middle western experience," which made them, "at least in the author's eyes, seem worthy themselves of preservation."[51] And this is, indeed, the extent of what later critics and historians would claim for them, sizable as that contribution was to the local-color movement. Price noted that "Mrs. Catherwood's forte was in recording a multitude of realistic human-interest details of manners, customs, speech, and every-day incidents," and that "within the compressed scope of the short story . . . she was able to integrate form and color with highly artistic results."[52]

Catherwood excelled at the short story because she excelled at depiction of the smallest and humblest detail and in vivid sensory images. In "Lilith," a three-part serial that appeared January–March 1881 in *Lippincott's Magazine*, Indiana fared little better than it did in the author's shorter fiction, as when she describes the odor of a typical Hoosier cabin. "The fragrance of liniments and hot vinegar mingled with a native odor of grease, producing a compound which seemed capable of being cut into blocks."[53]

"Lilith" is the story of a cultivated girl who, when orphaned, comes to Indiana to live with her uncle. The uncle, formerly of a more genteel background, has been slowly reduced in status, speech, and habits by the crudity of his environment. Much to Lilith's horror, he speaks in "the idiom of the country, which had slowly but surely incrusted him as lichen gathers on a fallen log: 'Did you see all them fellers 'at rode by here this evenin'? Where's they goin'?"[54]

The abuse of language was a frequent theme in Catherwood's fiction as in "T'Fergore," another of her Indiana stories, where in describing the narrator's brother she concedes that "he had an affectionate and honorable nature, and soon quit spitting upon our Brussels rugs and hard finished floors; his English, however, was beyond all help."[55]

Language was not the only distinguishing characteristic of Catherwood's rustics. In "The Fairfield Poet," "the male portion of the community sat on the railroad platform in yellow jeans, sprawling their naked toes to the sun, whittling, and jetting with the regularity of fountains."[56] Similarly, in "Mallston's Youngest," "the Fairfield loungers were famously lazy savages . . . the whole smoking, stoop-shouldered, ill-scented throng."[57]

Catherwood's grim perception of Fairfield, Indiana, was undoubtedly inspired to some extent by discontent in her marriage to James Steele Catherwood. The railway platform on which the local rubes lounge and expectorate was "the forlornist of Indiana railroad stations." In the story Catherwood's character "hated Fairfield as a background to her existence, but there had fate nailed her for life."[58]

Mary Hartwell Catherwood, one of Indiana's earliest authors and intimate of James Whitcomb Riley.

The Western Association of Writers. Catherwood helped establish the organization, along with Maurice Thompson and James Whitcomb Riley.

In "Mallston's Youngest" the schoolmistress, an aspiring writer, exclaims, "I want such different things—the society of the cultivated, the stimulus of great natures. . . . I never shall amount to anything with my surroundings."[59]

However happy or unhappy Catherwood's marriage might have been, Shumaker speculated about the nature of her relationship with Riley. When they met in 1879 both were less than contented, Riley as yet unrecognized and Catherwood regretting having "given up literature for marriage in an unloved country town."[60] Though she had not exactly "given up literature" as evidenced by the dates of her publications in various local newspapers, she did miss the modest success that she had enjoyed as a single woman in New York State and in Cincinnati.

The Catherwoods moved to Indianapolis in late 1879, where Riley had, coincidentally, just taken a newspaper position. While Mr. Catherwood labored in the confectionery business, Mrs. Catherwood was "quickly swept into the literary life of the city." She was in regular contact with all the literary figures of Indianapolis, and Shumaker notes that "the association with likeminded people must have greatly inspired her, because while she lived in Indianapolis her literary production was large."[61] With Riley and Maurice Thompson, among others, she helped establish the Western Association of Writers. One product of this period was the novel *Craque-O'-Doom*, which was named after one of Riley's poems. What Shumaker referred to as the "ripening friendship" between Catherwood and Riley "resulted in mutual literary inspiration, and they collaborated on several projects, among which was . . . a romantic story of the lives of two writers that, strangely, resembled theirs."[62] The project was abandoned. A small biography of Catherwood by M. L. Wilson, written in 1904, is silent on the subject of Riley. Of course, written in 1904 and by an acquaintance of Mrs. Catherwood, it praises the later romantic novels and neither mentions the Catherwoods' separation in 1899, nor the early works of critical realism.

Whatever the character of her relationship with Riley, it is probably true that it affected Catherwood's style of writing, which became decidedly more sentimental during the most intense phase of their friendship. Whether the evolution had anything directly to do with Riley, or everything to do with the move to an urban environment and the company of literary society, it is tempting to speculate that as her intimacy with Riley and other literary figures increased, her interests and goals in common with her husband might have decreased. Though the Catherwoods left Indianapolis in 1882 and lived together for another seventeen years, Mrs. Catherwood never again wrote about the Midwest or indeed wrote with any measure of realism. With the publication of her most popular novel, *Lazarre*, in 1901, her reputation became national in scope, while Mr. Catherwood persisted in plying in the pedestrian fields of postmastering and real estate.

Catherwood is barely known today for two romantic novels, *The Romance of Dollard* and *Lazarre*, perhaps because of what Pattee called "her failings as a romancer." He insisted, however, that she "must be reckoned with always as perhaps the earliest American pioneer of that later school of historical fiction writers that so flourished in the nineties." Because of Catherwood, Pattee contended, "*Alice of Old Vincennes* [Thompson] and *Monsieur Beaucaire* [Tarkington] . . . were foregone conclusions."[63]

Literary pioneers cannot help but "fail" by the standards of later generations. The same criticisms that were applied to Catherwood also were leveled against another early and more enduring Hoosier realist, Edward Eggleston. Weakness of plot and of structure, melodramatic conflicts with contrived resolutions, and a restrained realism limited by sentimentality and convention, all were failings of Eggleston and indeed of early realism as a movement.

Nevertheless, Ima Honaker Herron in *The Small Town in American Literature* counted Eggleston as one of four "Midland realists," along with Joseph Kirkland, E. W. Howe, and Hamlin Garland, "who chronicled . . . the difficulties of Western life" in a time when "the glamor of pioneering was gone and the visionary gleam was growing indistinct."[64] Ronald Weber, likewise, grouped these four in his critical study *The Midwestern Ascendancy in American Writing*. William Randel, in the Twayne U.S. Authors Series of critical biographies, referred to Eggleston merely as "one of a small group that redirected the course of American writing after the Civil War."[65]

Whatever the number of his peers, it is clear that the influence of Eggleston in both the areas of regionalism and realism cannot be overemphasized. As Weber put it, Eggleston "holds a place at the forefront of the turn toward realism as well as at the beginning of the serious literary interpretation of the Midwest."[66] Weber called it "an elementary Midwestern realism."[67] In the February 1971 issue of *The Markham Review*, Donald Kay called it "infant realism" and contended that, with all its weaknesses, *The Hoosier School-Master* was "the squawking child which gained the attention of the public and served as the forerunner of a new movement in American literature."[68]

Eggleston's principal contribution is difficult for the modern reader to appreciate, accustomed as we are to realism as well as to a sense of place in literature. It is easy to forget that prior to Eggleston no one had written about the frontier as a place peopled with ordinary, though colorful, characters, with a language, culture, and rich drama all its own. Eggleston preceded Twain, and prior to Eggleston no one had created realistic, interesting, subordinate characters, to say nothing of rustic characters. In the literature of Eggleston's generation, even peasants and slaves spoke in the dialect of the drawing room. *The Hoosier School-Master* was a new experience for the reader of Eggleston's era, steeped in the gentility and sentimentality of literary convention and accustomed to the literary stranglehold of the eastern seaboard.

Eggleston himself in the preface to *The Hoosier School-Master* admitted that "it used to be a matter of no little jealousy with us, I remember, that the manners, customs, thoughts and feelings of New England country people filled so large a place in books, while our life, not less interesting, not less romantic, and certainly not less filled with humorous and grotesque material, had no place in literature."[69]

Eggleston never had illusions of literary greatness and was always rather self-effacing about his contribution. "If I were a dispassionate critic," he wrote in a November 1890 article in *The Forum*, "and were set to judge my own novels as the writings of another, I should have to say that what distinguishes them from other works of fiction is the prominence which they give to social conditions; that the individual characters are here treated to a greater degree than elsewhere as parts of a study of a society—as in some sense the logical results of the environment. Whatever may be the rank assigned to these stories as works of literary art, they will always have a certain value as materials for the student of social history."[70]

Social history was, in fact, where Eggleston felt he would leave his legacy. He intended to write a series of social histories of the United States, though he lived to publish only two. In fact, it may be that his desire to promote history as a study of real people, rather than as a litany of battles and of dynasties, inspired him to write the kind of fiction that he did. If so, Eggleston denied that the process was conscious, adding, however, that "it is what we do without exactly intending it that is most characteristic."[71]

Most critics agree that Eggleston's novels, and particularly *The Hoosier School-Master*, have no abiding artistic merit. But most also agree that Eggleston's descriptions of midwestern rural life in the middle- to late-1840s are authentic and vivid, and later local colorists and realists acknowledge his influence. What Eggleston introduced in *The Hoosier School-Master* came, in its more polished forms, to define the very essence of American literature. "For Midwestern writers," Weber wrote, "coming from cramped or nonexistent literary backgrounds, the fragile new doctrine of truth-telling held special appeal."[72]

Undoubtedly, the financial success of *The Hoosier School-Master* had a rather special appeal as well. The novel appeared first as a short serial in the periodical *Hearth and Home* when Eggleston served as its editor and was to run in three installments. It was a desperate attempt, on Eggleston's part, to fill space and to offer something new and different in a faltering publication. Much to his surprise, the serial was so successful that he was hard put to keep up with the demand for more installments. Many of the novel's inherent flaws result from this very circumstance—that it was never intended to be a novel and was written piecemeal and under the pressure of a weekly deadline. In addition, Eggleston by

A rare candid photo of Edward Eggleston, author of The Hoosier School-Master.

A sketch of Edward Eggleston, who made it acceptable to write and read about Indiana.

his own admission had precious little exposure to the novel as a form and had no idea of how to structure one. Novel reading was not considered acceptable behavior in the strict Methodist home of his adolescence, and Eggleston would, for most of his life, harbor some feelings of guilt about authoring one. Hard as it is for contemporary readers to appreciate the societal, and particularly religious, constraints that helped shape the development of an American literature, the phenomenon was remarked upon by the critics of earlier generations. Pattee recognized as early as 1915 that Eggleston had "helped to create a new reading public, a public made up of those who, like himself, had had scruples against novel reading."[73] Effa Morrison Danner speculated in the *Indiana Magazine of History* in 1937 that the criticism and censure of the Methodist church may have kept Eggleston from becoming a true realist.[74]

Eggleston was born in Vevay, Indiana, in 1837 to a distinguished and well-educated family. His father was a lawyer and an Indiana legislator. After the father's death in 1846, Eggleston's mother married a Methodist preacher, and the family moved to New Albany. Eggleston, who suffered severe respiratory problems, worked for a time as a Bible agent and then rode a Methodist circuit. Though his health often interferred with his ministry, and though he occasionally dabbled in journalism, he never quite lost the calling, serving as pastor of a church in Brooklyn, New York, even after achieving success as a novelist. The fascinating story of Eggleston's struggles with faith and with the passions and pitfalls of organized religion can be gleaned from his novel *The Circuit Rider* and to some extent from *The End of the World*, a novel about the Millerite phenomenon. But for Hoosiers, Eggleston's chief interest lies in his vivid depiction of life on the Indiana frontier, which is captured best in *The Hoosier School-Master* and in *Roxy*, arguably his best work of fiction.

Frontier Hoosier character was so vividly captured in the latter two novels that the yokels first depicted by Eggleston quickly became something of a Hoosier "type," repeated not only in Catherwood and in Thompson's *Hoosier Mosaics*, but also in almost every novel and short story that has been written about the Indiana frontier. Eggleston denied that his characters were caricatures, though he also stressed that they represented a very small and select element of Indiana backwoodsfolk who had essentially, by the time the book was published, disappeared from the state. In fact, Eggleston had viewed them as an endangered species of sorts, the essence of which he wanted desperately to capture and preserve for future generations. Eggleston claimed that he had been familiar with exactly such characters and had witnessed their crude culture firsthand in long boyhood visits to an uncle's house in Decatur County, which was decidedly more rural and rustic than his native Vevay. It was here that he not only absorbed the dialect that he made famous in *The Hoosier School-Master*, but where he also witnessed the proliferation of yellow complexions, butternut jeans, straggling discolored teeth, and toothless grins. In both *The Hoosier School-Master* and *Roxy* Eggleston recorded the honored Hoosier pastime of tobacco spitting and the prevalence of superstition in the treating of "agur" and "yaller janders," of "cholery" and "rheumatiz" that he had witnessed firsthand. He described the schoolmaster boarding with the families of his scholars and "sleeping in a preoccupied bed, in the 'furdest corner,' with insufficient cover, under an insufficient roof, and eating floating islands of salt pork fished out of oceans of hot lard."[75]

"Whenever one writes with photographic exactness of frontier life he is accused of inventing improbable things,"[76] Eggleston wrote in *Duffels*, a later collection of stories. Interestingly enough, Eggleston's depictions of frontier life in the 1840s so mirrored those of Hall and Beecher that it would be hard to dismiss them as exaggeration. In the novel *Roxy* he not only reported the same sallow complexions, stump-strewn streets, and mud "only navigable to a man on a tall horse,"[77] but he also recorded, with indisputable similarity, the prejudice against "larnin'" that frustrated the educator and the struggle of frontier clerics to make a decent living. He even commented on the role of the minister's wife, "a person of seriousness and piety, one who can visit the sick, and get up female prayer-meetings and sewing circles." He cautioned that "a minister's wife should not talk too much. She ought to be quiet and grave," adding that "a minister's usefulness, you know, depends so much on his wife."[78]

The lack of enthusiasm for "larnin' " is, of course, the subject of *The Hoosier School-Master*. Set in "Hoopole Kyounty, State of Injeanny,"[79] this remarkable little book is based almost entirely on the experiences of the author's brother, George, when he was a schoolmaster in a rural school near Madison, Indiana. When Ralph Hartsook, the master, meets "old Jack Means," a trustee of the Flat Creek school district to which Ralph has just walked ten miles to apply, he is warned that "the boys have driv off the last two, and licked the one afore them like blazes."[80] He is informed further that "we a'n't none of your saft sort in these diggins. It takes a *man* to boss this deestrick. Howsumdever, ef you think you kin trust your hide in Flat Crick school-house, I ha'n't got no 'bjection."[81]

Another of Hartsook's constituency admonished him early that "lickin' and larnin' goes together. No lickin', no larnin', says I. Lickin' and larnin', lickin' and larnin'."[82]

Hartsook eventually wins his students' respect through persistence, diplomacy, and his own dignified brand of creative persuasion. In the process, of course, Hartsook acquires a degree of fondness for, or at least adaptation to, his uncouth environment. Soon upon his arrival Hartsook is cautioned about the unpopularity of "polite" speech through a story of "a poar Yankee schoolmaster, that said 'pail' instid of bucket."[83] Near the end of the book Hartsook meets his romantic interest, Hannah, "carrying her bucket of milk (they have no pails in Indiana)."[84] The schoolmaster learns as much as he manages to teach his scholars.

Eggleston made an undisputed contribution to regionalism and realism in American literature, but he made an equally fundamental contribution to Indiana literature by writing the first nationally acclaimed book about Indiana, thereby gaining Indiana, with all its provincialism, a measure of attention and infusing the state with pride of place. Despite a predictable amount of grousing by locals about the unflattering portrait of themselves and their community as it appeared in *The Hoosier School-Master*, there was a great deal of pride of ownership exhibited after its publication. After all, unlike either Hall or Beecher, Eggleston was a Hoosier! Eggleston validated writing about Indiana, which in some measure validated living in Indiana. People everywhere suddenly wanted to hear more about this fascinating territory and its quaint folk, and generations of Indiana authors were only too happy to oblige.

CHAPTER THREE

When Knighthood Was in Flower

The Indiana Romancers

In the late 1800s and early 1900s American literature was held hostage by a reading public raven-
ous for romantic and sentimental fiction. What is
remarkable for Hoosiers is that, for a substantial span of time,
Indiana was ground zero. Theories as to why this should have
been so abound, although none of them is particularly satisfying.

But regardless of the causes, the years 1870 to 1920, Indiana's
so-called golden age of literature, were, with the major exceptions
of Riley and George Ade, shaped primarily by Hoosier novelists.
Maurice Thompson, Lew Wallace, Booth Tarkington, Meredith
Nicholson, George Barr McCutcheon, Gene Stratton-Porter, and
Charles Major topped a list of best-selling authors who, for whatever reason, not only put Indiana on the nation's literary map with
a succession of exemplary works of romantic fiction, but in a very
real sense also defined the genre in American literature. Titles
such as McCutcheon's *Graustark* and Major's *When Knighthood
Was in Flower* quickly became the standards by which the
American romance novel was measured. Whatever the contemporary reader thinks about the form and regardless of the contempt
of many critics, most literary historians recognize Indiana's
golden age as a bona fide phenomenon in American letters and
acknowledge the impact of the Hoosier "romancers."

That literary historians mention the era at all is evidence of its
existence if not its influence. In *The New American Literature,
1890–1930*, Fred Lewis Pattee referred to "the high-tide period
. . . of the doublet-and-hose romance" and ranked Tarkington's
Monsieur Beaucaire as "perhaps . . . the best of them all."[1] Alfred

Kazin in *On Native Grounds: An Interpretation of Modern American Prose Literature* laments the demise of early realism contending that it was "submerged by historical romanticism and Stevensonian gush."[2] Realism, according to Kazin, had been "overrun by the tide of Graustark fiction."[3] That the term "Graustark fiction" should be understood to stand for the popular literature of an era is significant. And so while a critic of Kazin's stature dismisses the genre as "superplush fiction" and "historical confectionary,"[4] he still acknowledges the Hoosier school by elevating, as its principal perpetrators, George Barr McCutcheon and Charles Major.

The "tide" of historical romance ebbed and flowed with changing social and economic circumstances. Kazin notes that romanticism "flourished in prosperity and yielded dolefully to realism in periods of crisis and panic," but that it enjoyed "unparalleled confidence in the expansive years after the Spanish-American War."[5] This was, coincidentally, the same period in which a burgeoning interest in the Midwest, reflected in the popularity of *The Hoosier School-Master*, reached its zenith with the World's Columbian Exposition in 1893. Suddenly it was a source of pride to reside in the West, as well as to write about it. Suddenly it was possible to be an Indiana writer, hopeful of a national audience, and convinced of a legitimate subject matter.

This new Hoosier voice took two forms. Graustark fiction perfected a long literary tradition of exotic settings with elaborate costumes, courtly romance, and plenty of swordplay. But a new type of romantic novel, which began with the instant success of Tarkington's *The Gentleman from Indiana* and reached its height in Nicholson's *The House of a Thousand Candles* and Stratton-Porter's *A Girl of the Limberlost*, capitalized on local-color interest by utilizing familiar settings, contemporary circumstances, and ordinary characters, while adding the necessary elements of adventure, intrigue, danger, and romance. The near-Gothic atmosphere of Nicholson's Glenarm House evokes images of Jane Eyre, and Stratton-Porter's Limberlost Swamp is as mysterious, ethereal, and conducive to romantic interludes as any English moor.

While Indiana authors rode the crest of the romantic wave for several decades, and their romances were, for the most part, popular and profitable, all of the major Indiana romancers experimented, some to greater, some to lesser degrees, with realism, and with few exceptions their best work is to be found when they wrote honestly about their own state.

The notable exception is one of Indiana's earliest historical romance novels. In 1880 Lew Wallace published *Ben-Hur*, which quickly became and continues to be one of the most famous and widely read novels by an Indiana author, in addition to being made into one of the most popular and enduring films of all time. And yet Lew Wallace, unlike the other Hoosier romancers, never chose to write a novel, romantic or realistic, about Indiana, and therefore his body of work cannot be linked with the celebration of the Indiana scene represented by the other golden age romantic novelists. Not only did Wallace not write about Indiana, but he also did not really "live it," according to Meredith Nicholson. Nicholson, while recognizing Wallace's gift, called him "an oriental born out of his clime and time," and considered him "the least 'literary' " of Indiana authors.[6] Nicholson was not commenting upon Wallace's talent but upon his lifestyle, which did not include the swirl of literary activity in turn-of-the-century Indianapolis. Though he was acquainted with and associated with many of the other golden age authors, writing was, for Wallace, only a pastime. He embraced the life of a soldier, not that of a litterateur.

A writer very much at the center of Indianapolis literary life, however, was Mary Hartwell Catherwood, who very quickly followed Wallace as an early historical romance writer, and who, as discussed previously, also had the distinction of being a pioneer realist. In 1881 she published her first novel, *Craque-O'-Doom*, a semirealistic story set in Ohio. It was followed by *The Romance of Dollard* as early as 1889, a tedious romance set in Canada, and *Lazarre* in 1901. Though Catherwood's strength was as a realist and not as a romance writer, her work was a precursor for historical romance set proudly in the New World rather than in European courts and castles. Fortunately for today's readers and for Catherwood's own literary reputation, in the same year that she published *The Romance of Dollard* she also published *The Queen of the Swamp, and Other Plain Americans*, a collection of short stories, most of which had been appearing in periodicals for a number of years. The stories are all set in the Midwest and are grouped by state; two are set in Indiana. *The Queen of the Swamp* represents Catherwood's best work and the only fiction for which she still retains any real stature as an Indiana writer.

Indiana's first real romancer was Charles Major, whose enormously successful *When Knighthood Was in Flower* set the standard for historical romance in 1898 and gained him instant literary fame.

Though Major was born in Indianapolis in July 1856, his family moved to Shelbyville, where Major practiced law and spent the rest of his life, dying there in 1913. Like others of his literary circle, Major dabbled in politics, serving a term in the Indiana legislature. But his passion was English history, particularly that of the Tudors, and in a natural outgrowth of this passion he penned a fictional account of Mary Tudor's love affair with Charles Brandon, a commoner and favorite in the court of Henry VIII. Major wrote *Knighthood* under the pseudonym of Sir Edwin Caskoden, hoping to enhance its credibility and appeal by playfully masquerading it as the memoir of a court insider. Though the novel was first turned down by Harpers, Bowen-Merrill of Indianapolis published it in 1888. The company selected the title, taken from a poem by an English writer. It was an instant best-seller, and the author's identity was revealed. The story was dramatized both on stage and on film. The popular stage version was a huge success when it was performed in Indianapolis at English's Opera House in December 1900.

Following the overwhelming response to *Knighthood*, Major wrote half a dozen other period romances, including another best-seller, *Dorothy Vernon of Hadden Hall*. But it was his second book, *The Bears of Blue River*, that earned Major an enduring place in Indiana literature. A beloved Hoosier title that is still on bookstore shelves, it is a grizzly adventure story about young hunters obsessed with tracking and killing bears. The novel is set in Shelby County. The Big Blue River is real, making the book a staple in Shelbyville classrooms and in many other Indiana fourth-grade classrooms where it still stands as a classic of Indiana juvenile literature. What has also ensured its survival is the fast-paced and vivid depiction of one bloody encounter and conquest after another, particularly guaranteed to fascinate a young male audience.

Adult audiences of Major's day were by no means immune to the thrilling theme of victorious hunter against savage beast. Perhaps nowhere in American literature is the subjugation of nature more graphically depicted and celebrated than in this short book, where the level of gratuitous violence against bears is unsettling to contemporary sensibilities, particularly as the novel purports to be a first-rate adventure story for juveniles. There is something more fundamental in this theme than the pleasure of sport, something more revelatory than the thoughtless disregard for the sanctity of wildlife common to another period. There is in Major's book an unmistakable reveling in destruction that speaks to and satisfies a primal lust for the total conquest of nature. In *Landscape and Memory* Simon Schama reminds the reader that "unlike some modern ecological sensibilities, the old epics of the forest were not squeamish about the kill, experiencing it as a consummation, not a desecration, of woodland nature."[7] It could be argued then that Major's bravado is simply dated and politically incorrect like the images of blacks and women in early Indiana literature. In this novel the young hero Balser and his buddies live to hunt bear. Indeed, as if it were his great white whale, young Balser reckons time by the killing of the bear—before and after. In a series of harrowing adventures the boys test their courage and prowess against innocent creatures depicted as beasts to enhance the sense of danger and of justification. In almost every instance the boys deliberately court confrontation, once even invading a bear's tree lair for the night, knowing full well that the tree is inhabited. When the unsuspecting bear returns for the night, they rout and brutally butcher him. Then they "went over to the spot where the bear was lying stone dead with Balser's bullet in his brain. The dogs were sniffing at the dead bear, and the monster brute lay upon the snow in the moonlight, and looked like a huge incarnate fiend.

"After examining him for a moment the boys slowly walked back to the [hollow] tree. When they had entered they raked the coals together, put on an armful of wood, called in the dogs to share their comfort, hung up the deerskin at the door, drew the bearskins in front of the fire, and sat down to talk and think."[8] In this action the hunters have thoroughly violated, indeed domesticated, the bear's habitat, furnishing it with the spoils of their victory. On the one hand, in good pioneer fashion every part of the animal is made use of. On the other hand, to wrap one's self in the hide of the vanquished is the ultimate act of contempt. From that point on the boys called the tree "their 'Castle on Brandywine.' "[9]

The bear is allegorical, of course, a metaphor for the effrontery of savage nature whose resistance to subjugation must be punished. But what, then, about the fawn and doe that Balser happens upon "watching him intently with their great brown eyes"? Balser shoots the fawn, "knowing that if he did so, its mother, the doe, would run for a short distance and would return to the fawn . . . and so it happened that the doe and the fawn each fell a victim to our hunter's skill."[10]

The reader of nearly a century ago was supposed to view young Balser as a hero for "if he but possessed the coveted carbine he could, single-handed and alone, exterminate all the races of bears, wolves and wildcats that inhabited the forests round about, and 'pestered' the farmers."[11] Youngsters were expected to experience vicarious thrills as "Tom . . . struck the bear upon the head with the sharp edge of his hatchet, and chopped out one of his eyes,"[12] and as Balser shoots right into "the great red mouth."[13] The modern reader may decide never to acquaint his or her children with this particular "juvenile" gem.

More palatable, but also less popular, was another juvenile title utilizing many of the same characters, *Uncle Tom Andy Bill*. Aside from these two, Major attempted only one other novel set in Indiana. It was titled *A Forest Hearth: A Romance of Indiana in the Thirties*, and it was as unsuccessful as *Knighthood* was successful. The novel's lack of popularity probably was due to the fact that it was a contrived story, with an insipid, unappealing hero and heroine and rural folk who speak like English aristocrats. "I warn you there will be no heroics in this history," Major writes early in the text, "no palaces, no grand people—nothing but human nature, the forests, and a few very simple country folk indeed."[14] *A Forest Hearth* was published in 1903, well after *The Gentleman from Indiana* and *Alice of Old Vincennes*, and Major was hoping to tap into the deep well of Hoosier romantic hysteria. As evidenced by the popularity of such Indiana titles, the reading public was inspired by stories of simple country folk but did not respond to imitations of inferior quality. Still Charles Major can be appreciated for attempting to show that the human drama could be played out in an Indiana forest as rivetingly as in a renaissance court.

Following hard upon the heels of *Knighthood* was Tarkington's first novel, *Monsieur Beaucaire*. Though it was Tarkington's first, it was published after *The Gentleman from Indiana*, and its publication was, in fact, due to *Gentleman*, a happy accident that will be discussed in later chapters.

Gentleman is the story of a young easterner, John Harkless, who comes to the small Indiana town of Plattville to resurrect its newspaper, but who ends up rescuing the community from political corruption and the tyranny of the "White Caps," a hooded band of ruffians that has terrorized the locals for years. In the process he earns the love of the heroine and the respect and gratitude of everyone in Plattville. Finally, he is nominated for Congress, no small accomplishment for an outsider whose arrival in the town was greeted with suspicion because "people did not come to Plattville to live, except through the inadvertency of being born there."[15] In fact, the heroine expresses her admiration, but also her astonishment at Harkless's choice "to live here, out of the world, giving up the world."[16]

But Harkless, who had come to Indiana as a last resort career-wise, "finds himself," his love, and his life's work in Indiana. Though *Gentleman* is a sentimental romance with plenty of suspense and danger, it is also true to its setting, not sparing in its depictions of the "monotony" of the landscape, the "flat lonesomeness"[17] that Harkless finds so oppressive early in the story. By the end of the novel, predictably, the "far tinkling of farm-bells," has, in three short months, changed utterly in its effect upon Harkless. Whereas before "John Harkless had listened to that sound, and its great lonesomeness had touched his heart like a cold hand; . . . now, as the mists were rising from the water and the small stars pierced the sky one by one, glinting down through the dim, immeasurable blue distances, he found no loneliness in heaven or earth."[18]

As Harkless comes of age, so, too, does the town of Plattville, and its social and physical growth is tinged with a sense of impending loss of innocence. "Stagnation and picturesqueness will flee together; it is the history of the Indiana town."[19]

Tarkington entered American literature as a local colorist, though of a decidedly sentimental and romantic bent, rather than as a romancer. He would leave it as a realist and a social historian of some note, and for these reasons he is discussed in future chapters.

Maurice Thompson wrote at the same time and in much the same vein as Mary Hartwell Catherwood, and, like Catherwood, Thompson's best work was his semirealistic short fiction collected in *Hoosier Mosaics*, published in 1875. But, like many of his contemporaries, he is best remembered for a singular piece of romantic fiction published some twenty-five years later.

James Maurice Thompson was born in Fairfield, Indiana, in 1844; however, the family migrated to the South and he was residing in Georgia at the outbreak of the Civil War. The young Thompson served as a Confederate soldier and left the South shortly after the war, ending up in Crawfordsville, Indiana, where he eventually practiced law, being a partner for a time with Lew Wallace. He served in the state legislature in 1879. He died in Crawfordsville in 1901.

As a writer, Thompson was a decent poet and an above-average nature writer and, though he began and ended his career writing about Indiana, most of his fiction is set in the South, "full of magnolias and mockingbirds"[20] as Walter L. Fertig characterized it in the December 1964 issue of the *Indiana Magazine of History*. In fact Thompson has sometimes been classed as a southern writer, particularly because he addressed the issue of reconciliation between the North and the South in several novels. The semiautobiographical *A Banker of Bankersville*, set in the border-state ambiguity of Indiana, addresses this theme.

Although *Banker* sold well, Thompson did not enjoy success as a novelist until the publication of *Alice of Old Vincennes*, his last book, in 1900. *Alice* is the story of George Rogers Clark's victory at Fort Sackville. This blending of historical fiction, romance, and an actual, significant event in Indiana and American history, actually was commissioned by the Bowen-Merrill publishing company, rather than inspired by any real desire on Thompson's part to write a romance set in Indiana. The Bowen-Merrill Company was seeking a successor to *When Knighthood Was in Flower*, having recognized that though the public's taste for costume romances was still a lucrative market, readers were quickly developing a taste for romantic stories set in their own backyard. In addition, Bowen-Merrill had a vested interest in promoting Indiana writers, and so the company handpicked the setting, the subject, and the author of *Alice*.

It was a new era in publishing, with the novel enjoying a new acceptance and a profound popularity among a growing number of leisure readers. The idea of big-volume publishing and of actively promoting books and authors to increase sales was born. Whether by coincidence or design, this development was fortuitous for authors and responsible for the enormous and instant success of books such as *Knighthood* and *Alice*. Tarkington, meanwhile, was enjoying the same advantages though with a different publisher. While he was not the darling of a local house, still he was a Hoosier who had published almost simultaneously a best-selling foreign romance and a sentimental local-color story set in his home state. Both reader interests converged to make an exceedingly fertile ground for Indiana romance authors.

Alice of Old Vincennes was written in the South, and its romantic flavor undoubtedly was enhanced by Thompson's passion for his former climes. The novel is dedicated to an M. Placide Valcour of Louisiana, a descendant of one of the earliest French families of Vincennes, and Thompson's frequent host, in hopes that it would "always be connected with a breezy summer-house on a headland of the Louisiana gulf coast, the rustling of palmetto leaves, the fine flash of roses, a tumult of mocking-bird voices, the soft lilt of creole patois, and the endless dash and roar of a fragrant sea over which the gulls and pelicans never ceased their flight, and beside which you smoked while I dreamed."[21] In such an environment Thompson could hardly have written anything but a dreamy, romantic vision of Indiana in "the time that tried men's souls,"[22] markedly unlike the Indiana communities portrayed in his *Hoosier Mosaics*, one of which was described as "a place of some three hundred inhabitants, eking out an aguish subsistence . . . sucking like an attenuated leech at the junction. . . . It lay mouldering . . . slowly rotting in the swamp."[23] The Indiana of Thompson's earliest and best work was often the Indiana of mosquitoes and malaria, tobacco-chewing yokels, and coarse, sometimes characterless women, who were far different from the refined and virtuous Alice.

In 1901 a new romancer entered the literary scene when George Barr McCutcheon published *Graustark: The Story of a Love behind a Throne*. McCutcheon wrote half a dozen Graustark spin-offs before he began to write semirealistic fiction set in Indiana, which represents his best literary efforts. Still he was loved and is remembered for conjuring the mythical kingdom that loomed so large in the American imagination that it was sincerely believed by many readers to be a real place.

Like Charles Major, McCutcheon was an instant literary success with his first novel, though, unlike Major, he had served an apprenticeship in journalism prior to exploring fiction. Born near Lafayette, Indiana, in July 1866, he worked as a reporter and then as city editor for the *Lafayette Journal* and *Lafayette Courier*, respectively. He was an intimate, along with his brother John T. who became a famous illustrator and cartoonist, of Tarkington, Ade, and Nicholson.

Although McCutcheon primarily wrote romance, what one columnist called "good, clean fun,"[24] and loved the genre, he admired and aspired to write realism. He approached it in several of his novels, most evidently in his two novels set in Indiana, *The Sherrods* and *Viola Gwyn*. McCutcheon moved to New York in

1904 and died there in 1923. Ironically, he wrote his Graustark stories while working as a journalist in Lafayette, but he wrote his two Indiana novels while a resident of New York.

Graustark was believed to be an imitation of the enormously popular and influential *The Prisoner of Zenda*, though McCutcheon denied ever having read the popular novel by Anthony Hope, claiming to be inspired instead by Robert Louis Stevenson. Whether or not McCutcheon actually read the novel, he was indirectly influenced through the countless romance novelists whom he did read and admire and who had been influenced by *Zenda*. However derivative it might have been, *Graustark* became the measure thereafter and, in its own right, inspired any number of imitations, some of which were McCutcheon's own. The author was tremendously prolific, approaching Tarkington and Nicholson in terms of yearly output. McCutcheon's unique contribution to the mythical kingdom story, and perhaps what made him so popular with American audiences, was that his hero was an American, whose democratic brand of nobility wins the hearts of foreign nobles and commoners alike, and particularly that of the beautiful princess who is overcome with gratitude for the American's intervention into her country's domestic problems.

Graustark was followed in 1903 by two novels set in real-life America, *Brewster's Millions* and *The Sherrods*. Decidedly light reading, *Brewster's Millions* sold well and was made into a play. On the other hand, *The Sherrods* marked a real departure for McCutcheon coming as it did between *Graustark* and the Graustark progeny. Set in Clay Township, Indiana, *The Sherrods* is a sometimes intense psychological portrait of a bigamist, unusual and risky subject matter for 1903 audiences. In the novel Jud and Justine Sherrod are childhood sweethearts who marry. Justine, a schoolteacher, has inherited a small farm. Jud wants to be an artist, but being penniless, is forced to farm his wife's small estate. He continues to nurse his dream of becoming an artist, which puts him out of favor with the locals. "He cain't do a dasted thing but draw picters. His pap had orter walloped him good an' made him chop wood er somethin', 'stead o' lettin' him go on the

way he did. They do say he kin sketch things powerful fine. He
tuck off a picter uv Sim Brookses' sucklin' calves that was a daisy,
I've hearn. But that ain't farmin' by a dern sight."[25]

Jud's father was the wealthiest farmer in Clay Township before
a mining swindle ruined him and before "in an upstairs room of
the great old farmhouse, built by his grandfather when the country was new, he blew out his brains, unable to face the ruin that
fate had brought to his door."[26] This legacy of suicide rears its ugly
head later in the story.

Jud represents a civilized agrarian lifestyle. His antithesis Glen
Crawley, a drunk who stalks Justine and has threatened to kill
Jud, is the rugged frontier woodsman. Unlike Jud, "Crawley was
born in the dense timber land north of Glenville. His father had
been a woodchopper, hunter and fisherman. Hard stories came
down to town about Sam Crawley."[27] Interestingly, Justine's thirty-
acre farm is half timber and half cultivated, suggesting that she is
herself halfway between Glen Crawley and Jud Sherrod, wild and
tamed, and civilized and uncivilized.

One day Jud unexpectedly sells one of his sketches to a beautiful young Chicago society woman who is passing through. As a
result of the sale, Justine persuades Jud to go to Chicago to try to
establish himself as an artist. Though she is heartbroken to see
him go, the couple plans to reunite as soon as he establishes himself. In pleading her cause she is confident that "when you are
able, dear, to take me to you in the great city, we can be the hap-
piest people in the world. . . . You must not waste another day in
this wilderness."[28]

At first Jud is a fish out of water in Chicago. During his first
interview for a newspaper position he is asked to sketch a building and an elevated track across the street from the paper's offices.
"He felt uncertain, incompetent, uncomfortable, mainly because
he was to draw objects entirely new to his eye. It was not like
sketching the old barns and fences down in Clay Township."[29]

Jud quickly adapts to the challenges of city life and succumbs
to its seductions, and his lifestyle becomes progressively more
expensive and complicated as he enjoys more success and meets
interesting and sophisticated people. Not only does he postpone

the day when he might send for Justine to join him in the city, but he also sends her less and less money, and her economic situation becomes desperate. Indeed, Jud has never mentioned Justine to his new associates. "He had allowed his friends to believe him unmarried so long that it was next to impossible to explain."[30]

Predictably Jud is reunited with Celeste Wood, the young woman who bought his first sketch. Jud tries to pass off his interest in Celeste as gratitude. "She made you," a friend reminds him. "If it hadn't been for her, you'd be down there in the woods plowing hay and digging cucumbers and nobody'd know you were on earth."[31] Nobody, of course, but a faithful, loving wife. Jud visits Justine occasionally and is overcome with love for her and the desire to return to the "simple" life in the country. But when he returns to the city he is increasingly seduced by Celeste and her lifestyle until he finally asks her to marry him. "The power of his love [had] carried everything before it, sweeping honor and dishonor into a heap which . . . he called the mountain of happiness, and he resolved that it should be strong and enduring."[32]

Before his wedding to Celeste, Jud spends several days with Justine "utterly conscienceless, glorying in his love for her."[33] A mere week later he embarks on his honeymoon, writing to Justine that a kind benefactor is taking him to Europe to study. "But think of the wonderful things I'll have to tell you when I get back,"[34] he consoles her, meaning every word in his perverse sense of entitlement.

As their ship leaves the dock for Europe, Celeste exclaims, "We are at sea! We are at sea!" to which Jud responds slowly, "Yes . . . we are at sea."[35] In good naturalistic fashion, Jud accepts little or no responsibility for his predicament. "Almost unconsciously he had gone deeper into the mire of circumstances from which he could not now flounder." And so while Justine struggles to keep body and soul together on a deteriorating farm, "for four months Mr. and Mrs. Dudley Sherrod wandered over Europe. They saw Paris, Venice, Rome, Amsterdam, Brussels, Vienna."[36] Jud receives letters from Justine that he reads and rereads and kisses rapturously before he destroys them. He continues to adore Justine even as he plans to kill her in her sleep, to spare her heartbreak as well as to rid himself of the albatross of his past.

In this novel McCutcheon plays with the time-honored American literary themes of wilderness versus farm, farm versus city, and of an innocent cast adrift in the big city. But he also introduces the risky topic of marital infidelity and manages to paint a sympathetic portrait of a young man unable to control his sexual and material impulses. The ending of the novel, while not exactly a logical conclusion, is nonetheless unique in its resolution, and the fate of the two women who were Jud's victims is reminiscent of both *Sister Carrie* and *Jennie Gerhardt*. In all these respects McCutcheon anticipates Theodore Dreiser's *An American Tragedy* by twenty-six years.

While Jud is not a fully developed naturalistic figure, he is close enough to give McCutcheon credibility as something more than a romancer. In the December 1903 issue of *The Reader*, one insightful critic of the period put it this way: "In all things Mr. McCutcheon is one of the most modern of novelists, and in 'The Sherrods' he has epitomized the styles in fiction for 1903. In these piping days of degenerate morals we no longer believe in honest out-and-out heroes and villains. We know too well the goodness of a bad man and the badness of a good man, and the broad distinctions that once existed no longer hold good. . . . Equally is it true that 'The Sherrods' falls into none of the old convenient categories. It is neither a novel of manners, nor a psychological novel, nor a historical, romantic, realistic, social, or rural novel: but something of all these."[37]

McCutcheon's later novel *Viola Gwyn* is probably the most unflattering portrait of early Indiana to be produced by a Hoosier romancer. Viola and her father come from Kentucky and still are unprepared to face the rawness of life on the Indiana frontier. One of their first experiences is sharing a meal with a local who "ate largely with his knife, and smacked his lips resoundingly, swigged coffee from his saucer through an overlapping moustache and afterwards hissingly strained the aforesaid obstruction with his nether lip; talked and laughed with his mouth full,—but all with such magnificent zest that his guests overlooked the shocking exhibition." By way of explaining himself, the character says, "I got a week-day style of eatin' an' one strickly held back fer Sunday . . . same as clothes er havin' my boots greased."[38] The same fellow observes wryly that "there's setch a thing as bein' too danged clean, don't you think so? Sort o' takes the self-respect away from a man."[39]

The Gwyns settle in Lafayette where the calculated population includes dogs and where "a chaw of tobacco is as good as the state seal fer bindin' a bargain."[40]

By 1922 Hoosiers had grown accustomed to, and even somewhat proud of, such depictions of the early days of their state. The self-conscious mutterings that had greeted the far more benign images in *The Hoosier School-Master* and *The Gentleman from Indiana* had become a thing of the past.

Competing with Tarkington for the position as top literary figure in Indiana was Meredith Nicholson, a friend of Tarkington and of James Whitcomb Riley and well known throughout the literary communities of Indianapolis and Crawfordsville, where he was born in December 1866. As did so many of his fellow golden age authors, Nicholson practiced law for a time and dabbled in journalism before pursuing writing full time. Like Tarkington, his pursuit of writing was bankrolled—in Tarkington's case by a wealthy uncle, in Nicholson's by a wife of some means. Nicholson's first efforts were in poetry, and they were comparatively unsuccessful. His first novel, however, *The Main Chance*, published in 1903 by Bobbs-Merrill, was a best-seller, and he quickly followed it with another, *Zelda Dameron*, this one set in Indianapolis. The author considered both to be "very Howellsy."[41]

Zelda Dameron was not as successful as *The Main Chance*, but it hardly mattered. Nicholson had found his literary niche, realizing the profitability of churning out romance stories set in his beloved native state. In 1905 he intentionally capitalized on the popularity of imaginary-kingdom tales, admitting that "at this time there was a deluge of tales in imitation of Anthony Hope's 'Prisoner of Zenda.' It occurred to me to show if possible that a romantic tale could be written, without an 'imaginary kingdom,' with the scene in our own Indiana."[42]

Meredith Nicholson in his study at 1500 North Delaware Street, circa 1907. Born in Crawfordsville, Nicholson resided in Indianapolis his entire adult life.

The product of this experiment, *The House of a Thousand Candles*, by far Nicholson's most popular book and probably the only one much read today, succeeded admirably in the stated objective. The novel is a well-crafted Gothic tale that suffers little from its setting on Lake Maxinkuckee, in and around the town of Culver, Indiana, called Annandale in the book. In the preface to the novel Nicholson states that for some time he had had "a long-ing to write an adventure tale with an old-world atmosphere in a new-world setting,"[43] and that he had deliberated about the best way to achieve his desired effect. "In order to surround the lonely house on the lake with the necessary air of isolation and mystery I fixed upon winter as the appropriate season."[44] This was an interesting and effective choice and departed radically from the preponderance of Indiana romance novels set in the month of June. The winter season in Indiana lends itself easily to the dark-ness and light imagery that is central to the novel. In addition the story is loaded with the requisite devices of a grim, inscrutable butler, unaccountable footsteps in unknown parts of the house, "the closing of doors and drawing of bolts,"[45] underground passages, and a beautiful but mysterious girl who is the only power that can draw the protagonist out of his fortress and into life, reconciling him with his destiny in rural Indiana.

In the story John Glenarm, a young vagabond and profligate who has squandered his inheritance, receives word that he has inherited his grandfather's house and estate in Wabana County, Indiana, but that in order to claim it he must reside there for a year. "He probably thought the rustication would make a man of me," Glenarm grouses.[46] Economic necessity compels him to accept the terms. "I'm about to go into exile," he complains to his friend, "and I want to eat one more civilized dinner before I go." The friend asks where Glenarm is bound. "Not Africa again?" "No," Glenarm replies. "Just Indiana."[47]

Glenarm's antiquated images of the "wilderness" to which he thinks he has been condemned are confirmed by the isolation of the enormous estate that is separated from the rest of the community by dark, overgrown grounds and a high wall. The interior of the house, surprisingly "handsome and . . . marked by good taste in the midst of an Indiana wood," is lit by thousands of candles rather than by gaslight. Carved in the paneling of the house are the words, "The Spirit of Man Is the Candle of the Lord."[48] Although Glenarm finds this eccentricity disconcerting, he clings to the lighted interior of the house as his only refuge in what he perceives to be the darkness of the Indiana wilderness that surrounds him. Throughout the novel, safety and civilized society are found wherever lights shine. This perception effectively renders Glenarm trapped in his grandfather's estate so that the light circumscribes his loneliness, for "beyond the light of the candles lay a dark region that gave out ghostly echoes."[49]

Nicholson published a sequel to this novel in 1907, *Rosalind at Red Gate*, and several other adventure stories and light romances, a few of which were set in Indiana, but none of which was very successful. Then in 1912 he published *A Hoosier Chronicle*, considered by many, including the author, to be his best and most realistic novel. The novel is an attempt to depict realistically Indiana politics, detailing not only its chicanery and

maneuvering, but also its drama and glory. "For every one knows
that there is no hour of the day in any year when politics wholly
cease from agitating the waters of the Wabash."[50]

The novel is set in the fictional town of Montgomery
(Crawfordsville); the time "somewhat later than the second con-
sulship of Grover Cleveland and well within the ensuing period of
radicalism."[51] Nicholson uses the first chapter to apprise the
reader of numerous aspects of Hoosier life, not the least of which
is that "the Hoosiers with whom we shall have to do are not those
set forth by Eggleston, but the breed visible to-day in urban mar-
ketplaces, who submit themselves meekly to tailors and school-
masters."[52] He hastens to add that "no village is so small but it lifts
a smokestack toward a sky that yields nothing to Italy's," and that
it is "a soil more truly blessed than any that lies beyond the bor-
ders of [the] commonwealth."[53]

In an *Indianapolis News* article in September 1925 Nicholson
refers to the time depicted in the novel with more than a touch of
wistfulness. "A number of years ago I published a novel called 'A
Hoosier Chronicle,' in which I attempted to depict that older
Indianapolis to which many of us turn with affection, and with

*From an early deck of Indiana Authors
playing cards.*

regret for its passing. But the city's great industrial and commercial expansion has changed all that. There is no bringing it back."[54]

A Hoosier Chronicle revolves around the struggle to release the stranglehold political boss Morton Bassett has on the state. Dan Harwood, "fresh from college and with all the college-inspired ideals of clean, honest government,"[55] becomes Bassett's lieutenant and protégé; however, he is soon disillusioned with Bassett's underhanded political shenanigans. As Harwood begins to sense that his own ideals are slipping away from him, he manages to extricate himself from Bassett's camp and to foil Bassett's plans for higher office. The novel, however, ends happily for everyone concerned. The noble purposes of Harwood and Sylvia, the heroine, prevail, and the pair manages to redeem Bassett rather than to drive him from public life. The message of Nicholson's story is that the desire and capacity of Americans for self-government always prevails over dishonesty in politics and corrupt politicians. The novel concludes like a fairy tale. "It's all pretty comfortable and cheerful and busy in Indiana, with lots of old-fashioned human kindness flowing round; and it's getting better all the time. And I guess it's always got to be that way, out here in God's country."[56]

A Hoosier Chronicle was followed by a dozen other novels by Nicholson, of which *Otherwise Phyllis* and *The Proof of the Pudding* are worth reading for their Indianapolis setting. *Otherwise Phyllis* also is interesting for its unusual portrait of two uncommon women. Phyllis is a tomboyish young woman who was abandoned by her mother and has grown up alone with her father. She is tough, outdoorsy, and perennially tanned. "Phil's general effect was of brownness. Midwinter never saw the passing of the tan from her cheek; her vigorous young fists were always brown; when permitted a choice she chose brown clothes: she was a brown girl."[57] Phil, it should be noted, uses those "vigorous, young fists" upon occasion.

One day Phyllis's mother, Lois, unexpectedly returns to the small town she scandalized so many years before. Although Lois is regarded in her community as a shameless woman, as she would have been by most readers of Nicholson's era, she is a curiously sympathetic character, a gentle, thoughtful woman who admits that "there is no real soul in me. . . . I believe I am incapable of deep feeling: I was born that way."[58] After gaining the love and loyalty of her grown daughter, she again drifts out of Phyllis's life explaining that "you wouldn't love me much longer if I stayed! . . . You've seen the best of me. . . . I don't wear well, Phil."[59] Nicholson regarded Lois as "the best woman character I have done,"[60] though not his favorite. His favorite was the formidable Aunt Sally in *A Hoosier Chronicle*.

An equally unusual, though predominantly unsympathetic, mother is found in *A Girl of the Limberlost*, written by the last, but by no means the least, of the Hoosier romancers. Gene Stratton-Porter made her debut as a novelist and a romancer with a short novel about two cardinals. Her first substantial romance, *Freckles*, was published in 1904 and was set solidly in Indiana. It was followed by *A Girl of the Limberlost* in 1909 and other Indiana romances that made her one of the nation's best-loved and most successful authors. Though her best-selling novels were highly romantic Stratton-Porter is more effectively discussed within the context of agrarian literature. She was her most prolific toward the end of the romantic era when her fiction evolved into a form of rural realism, and, as with the other Hoosier romancers, Stratton-Porter's best literary efforts were realized when she wrote about Indiana life with some degree of realism. Stratton-Porter also belongs with the agrarians because her first love was nature writing and because it was her clear objective to promote the preservation of the physical landscape that inspired and infused her novels. Others of her contemporaries had been more concerned with preserving a vanishing social milieu and promoting an urban ideal.

Keith J. Fennimore wrote of Tarkington's *The Gentleman from Indiana* that it "presented American life as the vast citizenry would like to conceive it."[61] This sentiment could be applied equally to other golden age authors as well who, at a time when other American writers were profoundly influenced by the rise of naturalism, chose to meet the demands of a public whose taste in literature was verbalized by Alice in *Alice of Old Vincennes*: "I don't enjoy reading about low, vile people and hopeless unfortunates; I like sweet and lovely heroines and strong, high-souled, brave heroes."[62] Later in the narrative, referring to a particular novel that she is "caught" reading, Alice states that "sometimes it seems as if it lifted me up high above all this wild, lonely and tiresome country, so that I can see far off where things are different and beautiful."[63]

Even Theodore Dreiser, the Hoosier author who was considered to be the foremost creator of those "hopeless unfortunates," acknowledged the appeal of escapist literature in his last novel, *An American Tragedy*. Near the end of the story the character Clyde Griffiths tries to read for diversion in his prison cell where he is awaiting execution for the murder of his pregnant girlfriend. "His was a mind that, freed from the miseries that had now befallen him, was naturally more drawn to romance than to reality. Where he read at all he preferred the light, romantic novel that pictured some such world as he would have liked to share, to anything that even approximated the hard reality of the world without, let alone this."[64]

Regarding the romancers Kazin suggests that "but for a series of happy accidents, and the obvious taste of the new public for majestic writing and a fiction that glittered in epigrams, they might never have enjoyed their triumphant success."[65] And yet the case can be made, as William E. Wilson did admirably in *Indiana: A History*, that while most Hoosier novelists never would have achieved prominence as novelists if there had not been such a category as "the Indiana Author," more of them might have achieved "a taller stature as literary figures" without that label.[66]

CHAPTER FOUR

The Mark of the Machine

The Indianas of Tarkington and Dreiser

Largely as a challenge to the enormous popularity of romantic fiction at the turn of the century that seemed to serve no purpose other than to idealize historical events and exotic locales, a new generation of young American writers, heavily influenced by William Dean Howells, sought to portray "real life," to dramatize the everyday, the commonplace, and the ordinary experiences of average Americans, as they saw them.

The early realists were concerned with documenting social customs and domestic routines and with capturing the sights, sounds, and smells of their time and place. They were not concerned with exploring large social issues, and as the heirs of literary convention, they were anything but morally objective.

Newton Booth Tarkington was Indiana's chief practitioner of this brand of "gentle" realism, tinged as it was with sentimentality and genteel values. He was born in Indianapolis in 1869 and died there in 1946. With the exception of keeping a summer home in Kennebunkport, Maine, in the later years of his life, Tarkington remained a resident of Indianapolis his entire life. He lived for forty-six years at 1100 North Pennsylvania Street, attended Shortridge High School and, briefly, Purdue University. He served in the 1903 Indiana General Assembly and died in his home at 4270 North Meridian Street, the only one of his Indianapolis residences that still stands. More important, he wrote about his state and his city with warmth, humor, and genuine affection.

The fact that he not only wrote about Indiana, but that he also chose to live there, may have everything to do with his enormous

Booth Tarkington's last Indianapolis home, at 4270 North Meridian Street, still a private residence.

popularity within the state. He shares this attribute with other Indiana golden age authors, many of whom contributed to a literature not so much of local color, but of unabashed boosterism. Because of the success of *The Hoosier School-Master* and the enormous popularity of Riley's poetry, it suddenly had become not only respectable to be a Hoosier and to write about it, but also lucrative. Meredith Nicholson, Tarkington's contemporary, friend, and a prolific novelist in his own right, was the most ardent defender of the Hoosier State. Nicholson addressed the subject directly in numerous essays and magazine articles, wrote a small but valuable book about Indiana authors called *The Hoosiers*, and managed to incorporate a defense of the Hoosier lifestyle and letters into a number of his novels.

Nicholson, perhaps even more than Tarkington, dealt with the theme of wandering native sons who returned to the home place with new perspectives. In an essay entitled "Stay in Your Own Home Town," he poked fun at his fellow Hoosier author and friend. "Tarkington wanders a great deal, but Thanksgiving always finds him carving turkey in his home town where 'Penrod' lives."[1] The novel *Otherwise Phyllis* is Nicholson's most direct articulation of his philosophy of writing. The novel is essentially a celebration of the peace and prosperity to be found in staying where you are and writing about what you know.

Nicholson, for all his prodigious output, never approached Tarkington in popularity. If Tarkington was not Indiana's most gifted author, he was unquestionably the state's most versatile and prolific writer, having published some three dozen novels, two dozen plays, and countless short stories, essays, and articles, as well as respected juvenile literature, including the beloved Penrod stories.

Tarkington burst upon the literary scene in 1899 with *The Gentleman from Indiana*, a romance set in Indiana that has some value as local color. In fact, it is somewhat reminiscent in theme and style of *The Hoosier School-Master*. Tarkington actually intended the novel to be a vindication of his native state after having spent years defending its virtues to his classmates at Phillips Exeter Academy and Princeton University. As with *The Hoosier School-Master*, its publication was greeted with some mild grumbling about Tarkington's portrayal of certain local types but, in general, Hoosiers were thrilled to see another book about Indiana achieve national literary prominence.

The publication of Tarkington's *Monsieur Beaucaire*, pure costume romance in a foreign setting, although written earlier, rode the coattails of *The Gentleman from Indiana*. The story goes that Tarkington's faithful sister, Hauté, carried the manuscript of *Monsieur Beaucaire* with her on a trip to New York where she tried, unsuccessfully, to market it to S. S. McClure, of *McClure's Magazine*. When she mentioned, more or less as a last-ditch effort, that the author had just completed work on another novel, this one set in Indiana, the publisher asked to see it instead, and the rest is literary history.

Tarkington followed *Beaucaire* with several light romances about what could be called the pleasantries of life in Indianapolis. Despite the popularity of *Beaucaire*, with its foreign setting and subject matter, Tarkington discovered with the success of *Gentleman* that greater gold could be mined in his own backyard.

Tarkington's backyard was solidly upper-middle class. He was born to a prosperous Indianapolis attorney and judge and to a mother of respectable New England ancestry, whose brother was a governor of California and a United States senator. A legacy from this uncle bankrolled Tarkington's early literary efforts while his friends and neighbors waited patiently for the young man to "do something."

Though both parents were well educated and Tarkington had the opportunity of an Ivy League education, he was never a serious student. Always democratic in their lifestyle choices, the Tarkingtons sent Booth to Exeter after a period of truancy from Shortridge High School, and he moved on to Princeton after two rather unremarkable years at Purdue University. Arthur Shumaker characterized Tarkington's university days as "a prolonged frolic,"[2] and critical biographer Keith J. Fennimore referred to his having "majored in extracurricular activities."[3] However formative these "activities"—including campus publications and theatrical productions—might have been, Tarkington's academic career was undistinguished, and he failed to graduate. He did, however, have a grand good time, a talent he exhibited throughout his life.

Tarkington resisted the temptation to drift into a career in journalism and endured his share of rejections as a freelancer, albeit safely under the umbrella of his uncle's bequest. With the publications of *Gentleman* and *Beaucaire*, however, he began a long and financially rewarding career, which remains impressive and enviable even by contemporary standards. Critics of Tarkington often have alluded to his privileged background and financial good fortune as the reason for his inability totally to embrace realism, his greatest liability as a literary figure. For today, despite his continued popularity in Indiana and two Pulitzer prizes, Tarkington is generally acknowledged to have been a writer whose value was purely in entertainment. In the *Indianapolis News* in 1939 one critic acknowledged ruefully that "Tarkington cheated himself of immortality by not thinking and writing about ugly things in an ugly way and by rejecting a philosophy of despair."[4] Nevertheless, he was hugely popular in his lifetime, writing what biographer

A young Booth Tarkington, probably about the time of his Purdue/Princeton days.

Robert C. Holliday called in the vernacular of the time "the type of native novel which was all the go with us."[5]

Tarkington's Indiana was characterized by unpretentious prosperity, stability, comfort, neighborliness, virtue, and goodwill. In a series of biographical articles that appeared in the *Saturday Evening Post* in 1941 Tarkington, recalling his Pennsylvania Street home, resurrected the mythic image of an entire society.

> Our house, shrouded in the ivies and Virginia creeper that my mother and father loved, loomed in the warm night under an Indiana moon, and all the neighborhood would be scented by the wild-crab tree in bloom in our back yard. On the side porch that was veiled by drooping vines, my father would sit reflective behind the garnet spark of his cigar. From the distance there'd be heard the cries and laughter of children playing Hi-spy after dark, and from the street the soft plod-plod of horses' hoofs on wetted dust as a family carriage or a surrey or phaeton lightly rumbled by, out for the evening drive. . . . Under the moons of those summer nights all was well. Throughout the town and throughout the wide quiet countryside beyond, men rested after the hot day and with easy hearts thought of the morrow. No one was anxious for America; and all through the world—except, perhaps, where sporadic tribesmen raided on the Congo—there was peace.[6]

This boyhood home memorialized by Tarkington was eventually razed for a parking lot.

Despite the arcadian images that made his novels so pleasant to read, Tarkington was not exempt from personal problems. The years 1903 to 1911 were marked by ill health, a failing first marriage, and alcoholism. In addition, he found himself unable to write anything substantial. In 1903, after recuperating in Kennebunkport from typhoid fever contracted at French Lick, Indiana, he began an eight-year period of wandering in Europe, with occasional forays into New York, where a lifelong flirtation with the theater blossomed into a serious affair. Finally, in 1911 he returned to Indianapolis and to a year of recovery, remarriage, and renewed interest in prose fiction.

But the Indianapolis of 1911 was markedly different from the Indianapolis of Tarkington's youth. He returned to find that his beloved city had been irrevocably changed by the industrial age. It had become, in a few short years, crowded, noisy, and, above all, dirty.

Biographer James Woodress stresses the profound influence of the dirtiness and notes that the Indianapolis of Tarkington's youth "had been blessed with abundant supplies of natural gas,"[7] but that the new industrial machine was powered by soft coal. By the time Tarkington returned, coal dust clouded the sky and blanketed the city. The effects of industrialization on both the landscape and the human psyche became for Tarkington the impetus for his major work, and smoke became his dominant metaphor.

Tarkington found his real voice when he began to write the social literature for which he is most regarded. The early romances too often offered little more than what Vernon Louis Parrington referred to as pleasant tales about the "courtship of nice young people through the agencies of parties and picnics."[8] This is a slight oversimplification. *The Conquest of Canaan*, for example, is a solid step in the direction of critical realism with its humorous but unflinching portrayal of small-town gossip, pettiness, and insularity. Regardless, Tarkington achieved substantial critical attention only after he began documenting the serious social changes that were transforming his own personal environment.

The *Growth* trilogy, comprised of *The Turmoil*, *The Magnificent Ambersons*, and *The Midlander*, along with the novel *Alice Adams* mark Tarkington's major period. *Alice* was originally conceived as the third book of the trilogy, but upon its completion seemed to stand apart from the heavy social themes of the first two novels, and so Tarkington concluded the trilogy with *The Midlander*.

The *Growth* novels are family sagas set in Indianapolis, though Tarkington never refers to the city by name. They span roughly the period from the turn of the century to the First World War, the end of the horse-and-buggy era and the dawn of the automobile age, reflecting the difficulties of that transition. Tarkington had

witnessed phenomenal social change in his lifetime. He had seen
Indianapolis grow rapidly from an oversized country town with
something like a market economy to a good-sized industrial city,
and what had happened in Indianapolis had happened in comparable cities throughout the Midwest.

Tarkington, like his characters, struggled with reconciling the
old and new social orders. He had seen his own stately and arbo-
real neighborhood sullied beyond recall by industrial pollution. He
had watched the commodious lawns being divided up into ever
smaller lots and the magnificent old residences becoming board-
inghouses and funeral parlors. During the year that he wrote *The
Midlander* Tarkington left his beloved Pennsylvania Street home
and moved to the suburbs (North Meridian Street at the time), the
same move that many of his characters would also make. On the
first page of *The Midlander*, Tarkington notes that the magnificent
old houses had been built to withstand "time, fire, and tornado"—
everything but progress.[9]

The Midlander is the story of a young man who dreams of pur-
chasing an old farm some distance from the city, getting the
streetcar lines to run out to it, and then selling off the lots for new
homes. Dan Oliphant is depicted as a visionary rather than as an
avaricious opportunist because his objective is not fundamentally
self-serving. He sees his new addition as being a way for the average wage earner to escape the growing ugliness in the heart of the
city. The conservative town fathers who thwart him at every
opportunity are depicted as shortsighted and self-serving.

The Midlander was in many respects Tarkington's attempt to
put a positive face on the inevitable. It was his answer to *The
Turmoil*, his earlier indictment of the blind pursuit of prosperity
and growth. *The Turmoil* is the story of James Sheridan, "the
biggest builder and breaker and truster and buster under the
smoke . . . the city incarnate,"[10] who, for all his material success,
remains a barbarian. And it is the story of Bibbs, his youngest son,
who, dreamy and in poor health, is "a failure as a great man's
son."[11] Speaking of his father to the girl next door, Bibbs laments,
"He's like a Hercules without eyes and without any consciousness
except that of his strength and of his purpose to grow stronger.

Stronger for what? For nothing."[12] The qualities that Bibbs attributes to his father apply, of course, to the city itself.

The Turmoil begins like a fairy tale. "There is a midland city," the opening lines read, "in the heart of fair, open country, a dirty and wonderful city nesting dingily in the fog of its own smoke."[13] The curious juxtaposition of dirtiness and wonderfulness reflects Tarkington's own conflicted feelings about the two faces of economic development. A short generation before, he laments in *The Turmoil*, "no one was very rich; few were very poor; the air was clean, and there was time to live."[14] Now the city "strove and panted."[15]

In a vivid scene Bibbs passes the new industrial sector of the city in his car, "two great blocks of long brick buildings, hideous in all ways possible to make them hideous; doorways showing dark one moment and lurid the next with the leap of some virulent interior flame, revealing blackened giants, half naked, in passionate action, struggling with formless things in the hot illumination."[16]

The elder Sheridan's impression of the smoke is that it is "good, clean soot; it's our life-blood, God bless it!"[17] And when asked by a visitor about how the women see it, James Sheridan "laughs uproariously. 'They know it means new spring hats for 'em!' "[18]

The Turmoil was followed in 1918 by *The Magnificent Ambersons*, which won a Pulitzer prize. It was made into a film by Orson Welles and earned several Academy Award nominations in 1942, including that for best picture. In *The Magnificent Ambersons* Tarkington painstakingly chronicles the decline of an old, aristocratic family as industrialization changes the social and economic character of its small midwestern community. Third-generation George Minafer is contemptuous of his widowed mother's interest in a successful automobile manufacturer, Eugene Morgan, though Minafer is willing enough to pursue the man's daughter. A self-made man, Morgan represents changes in the social order that Minafer cannot accept. As the Ambersons' little town changes into a sprawling city, whose industrial sections encroach upon the once-exclusive neighborhoods, the Amberson fortune evaporates; their "magnificence" becomes obsolete.

In this new social order "old times," just like "old money," count for very little and are even the subject of ridicule. " 'Old times?' Morgan laughed gaily from the doorway. 'Not a bit! There aren't any old times. When times are gone they're not old, they're dead! There aren't any times but new times!' "[19]

All three of the *Growth* novels, which could have been realistic novels, were shortchanged by Tarkington's penchant for happy endings. In *The Magnificent Ambersons* young George is redeemed by the necessity of taking up honest work, by which means he is reconciled with Morgan and with the daughter. In this way the marriage of the old and new social orders is finally achieved. That this is brought about, in part, by supernatural means makes it even less palatable. But if George gets better than his character deserves, Keith Fennimore contended, it is because "he must remain as the pivotal figure between a benighted past and an enlightened future."[20]

The resolution is even more abrupt and unsatisfying in *The Turmoil*. Bibbs Sheridan becomes a successful businessman and reconciles with his father, but at the cost of his own artistic dreams and values, becoming profoundly disillusioned. Yet within three pages he is completely transformed by the love of a good woman. Although being reunited with the girl next door makes all of Bibbs's compromises and sacrifices seem worthwhile to him, the reader is left wanting.

The Midlander ends with the death of the hero. While it is not a happy ending, it is a decidedly romantic one. Dan Oliphant has worked himself to death for a better tomorrow and the greater good of his community, and the girl he loved marries his brother and goes to live in Dan's own beloved addition. "The new house was a white house, and it remained almost white; for the smoke reached it but thinly. . . . Shrubberies lived there, not suffocated; it was a place where faces stayed clean, children throve, and lilacs bloomed in transparent air."[21] In the last sentence of the book the young bride stands with her husband and surveys the now *distant* smoke. "Listen!" she importunes him. "That murmur of the city down yonder—why, it's almost his voice!"[22]

The *Growth* novels are marked by Tarkington's ambivalence about the social change he was witnessing everywhere around him. On the one hand growth was positive, indeed essential to a healthy society and economy. On the other hand unbridled materialism and bigness for the sheer sake of bigness can be a recipe for social and spiritual disaster. This dichotomy is reflected in all of Tarkington's fiction, but it is particularly evident in the trilogy. In this respect the *Growth* novels can be seen as cautionary tales.

In 1921 Tarkington published *Alice Adams*, which earned him his second Pulitzer. Though there are similarities between this novel and the trilogy, it is less a social comment and more a tragicomic portrait of a young woman in a constant frenzy of social climbing. Alice's family manages on the father's income, but Alice and her mother so covet the "advantages" that everyone else in town seems to enjoy that they cannot leave the beleaguered old fellow alone. Whereas Mrs. Adams constantly berates him and calls him a failure, Alice uses daughterly charm and manipulation to coax him into starting his own business. " 'Poor old papa! . . . He doesn't need to have everybody telling him how to get away from that old hole he's worked in so long and begin to make us all nice and rich. *He* knows how!' Thereupon she kissed him."[23] It is the kiss of a Judas because old Adams, compelled to leave the security of a company where he is valued and respected, is ruined.

Alice's life is a charade calculated to impress potential suitors. The novel is something of a series of episodes, humorous yet wrenching in their pathos. Alice pretends to live places other than her home. At a party that she has virtually crashed, she wanders "aimlessly through the rooms," on her brother's arm, "though she tried to look as if they had a definite destination, keeping her eyes eager and her lips parted;—people had called jovially to them from the distance, she meant to imply, and they were going to join these merry friends."[24]

Alice gestures, poses, laughs "airily,"[25] and "coquettes" exhaustively, all to no avail. Everyone eventually becomes wise to her game. One need only read the dinner party scene to get a vivid impression of the hapless Alice and her situation. The reader scarcely knows whether to laugh or cry.

By the end of the book Alice has grown immeasurably. The family has been forced to take on boarders, and although Alice has accepted the new reality, her mother has not. "I don't suppose we'll mind having any of 'em as much as we thought we would," Alice assures her mother. When mother tries to get her daughter to admit that she hates their situation, Alice responds, "No. . . . There wasn't anything else to do."[26]

Ultimately Alice is forced to enroll in Frincke's Business College, "that portal of doom."[27] Even in this final indignity, there is the opportunity for renewal and redemption.

> How often she had gone by here, hating the dreary obscurity of that stairway; how often she had thought of this obscurity as something lying in wait to obliterate the footsteps of any girl who should ascend into the smoky darkness above! Never had she passed without those ominous imaginings of hers: pretty girls turning into old maids "taking dictation"—old maids of a dozen different types, yet all looking a little like herself.
>
> Well, she was here at last! She looked up and down the street quickly, and then, with a little heave of the shoulders, she went bravely in, under the sign, and began to climb the wooden steps. Half-way up the shadows were heaviest, but after that the place began to seem brighter. There was an open window overhead somewhere, she found, and the steps at the top were gay with sunshine.[28]

Through the honor accorded his four major novels Tarkington achieved a reputation as a social historian, and his two Pulitzer prizewinning novels, *The Magnificent Ambersons* and *Alice Adams*, particularly, survive as rich portraits of a community in transition, a community that symbolizes the urban Midwest at the rise of the industrial age. In these works Tarkington recorded in the meticulous detail born of firsthand knowledge styles of dress and of deportment and details of architecture and of home furnishings of the period. He left invaluable records of music, cuisine, leisure activities, and popular literature. Though Tarkington provided accurate and illuminating descriptions of his physical and

The creator of Penrod *and* Alice Adams *at his desk.*

social environment, his sense of decorum concerning human behavior and motivation limited him as a realist, and his persistent romantic strain added an ephemeral quality even to his best work. Nevertheless, he remains Indiana's favorite literary son.

If Tarkington is the favorite son, Theodore Dreiser is the stepson about whom nobody talked until recently. Tarkington and Dreiser were close contemporaries. They were born slightly less than two years apart, within seventy miles of each other, and they both died in 1946. They published their first novels within months of each other. And yet they could not have been farther apart in their experiences of Indiana and in their reception as writers and as Hoosiers within the state.

Dreiser, whose name has become synonymous with the naturalist movement in American literature, was born in Terre Haute in 1871. He was the consummate social and literary outsider. Though Dreiser spent almost all of his formative years in Indiana, he has been traditionally ignored as an Indiana author. This exclusion has been attributed, variously, to the fact that he spent only his childhood in Indiana, that he did not stay in or return to Indiana to live, and that he did not write about Indiana. While the first two considerations are true, they are also true for other writers who have been included in the Hoosier canon. The remaining criterion for exclusion is simply not true. Dreiser wrote a good deal about Indiana in his nonfiction, and though Indiana was not the setting for any of his novels, his most important fiction was shaped profoundly by his experiences growing up there.

The naturalist movement was a logical product of the growing complexity of American society, which, naturalists believed, rendered the individual powerless and isolated. As a literary school, naturalism was a product of an immigrant, industrial, and urban society. The city had replaced the frontier as proving ground; so had the financier replaced the pioneer in the public's imagination. The labor-capital struggle became the new focus of romantic discontent, and economic worth the proof of fitness to survive.

For Dreiser the "city" was Chicago, a town already feeling its oats following the 1893 Columbian Exposition. With this formative event, the East had been supplanted as the center of the uni-

Tarkington with beloved poodle.

Dust jacket for Booth Tarkington's Penrod.

verse in the eyes of midwesterners, and Chicago, which would retain something of the aura of The White City long after the spectacle ended, never lost its wonder and its awesomeness for Dreiser. "The city of which I am now about to write never was on land or sea," he wrote in the autobiography *Dawn*. "Or if it appears to have the outlines of reality, they are but shadow to the glory that was in my own mind. . . . The city of which I sing was not of land or sea or any time or place. Look for it in vain! I can scarcely find it in my own soul now."[29]

Blanche Housman Gelfant contends in *The American City Novel* that "while other novelists of his time shared some of his isolated insights into the meaning of city life, none had gone through the total experience of discovery that gave Dreiser an inclusive and immediate knowledge of the modern city."[30] That "total experience" was the direct result of the extremes of environment that characterized Dreiser's early life, extremes that were absent in Tarkington's Indiana.

Tarkington grew up among the country club and cotillion set, while Dreiser grew up in crushing poverty. Tarkington had access to good schools, while Dreiser's early education was sometimes interrupted "for want of shoes"[31] and colored by demoralizing experiences in bleak parochial schools. And though Dreiser spent a year at Indiana University, it was only through the generosity of a former teacher who saw his potential.

While Tarkington enjoyed a close relationship with loving parents and a single sibling all his life, Dreiser lived in an unstable home. His father, John Paul, was unable to support his family of ten children. He was a brooding, humorless Roman Catholic and a severe disciplinarian who instilled a total repugnance for religion in Theodore, leaving him virulently anti-Catholic.

Theodore had a loving, illiterate, and rather dreamy and unconventional mother. She moved the children from one unsuitable environment to another; at one time they lived in a house of ill-repute in Evansville. The family, which was usually divided, lived at various times in Terre Haute, Evansville, Vincennes, Fort Wayne, Sullivan, and Warsaw, as well as, briefly, Chicago.

Tarkington enjoyed the luxury of independent means while he established himself as a writer. Dreiser worked a number of menial jobs before finally drifting into journalism, and he was influenced greatly by the underside of urban life that he witnessed as a reporter and by the journalistic style of the period.

In 1900 Dreiser published his first novel, *Sister Carrie*, arguably the most important literary event connected with the Hoosier State. Though the novel and its author suffered numerous indignities on the road to publication, *Sister Carrie* was destined to change the face of American literature.

The publication of *Sister Carrie*, so pivotal an event in American literary history, was something of an accident. The novel was accepted for Doubleday, Page and Company by editor Frank Norris, who recognized its significance. However, it was then withdrawn by Frank Doubleday himself, who felt that it dealt too candidly with delicate subject matter. Being legally obligated to release it, however, the company deliberately underprinted and undermarketed it.

Though a handful of critics and authors trumpeted *Sister Carrie*'s importance, numerous critics and an unreceptive reading public rejected its stark realism and its lack of a moral perspective. "What damaged Dreiser most in *Sister Carrie*," wrote William E. Wilson in *Indiana: A History*, "was that he violated the Genteel Tradition and wrote about poverty and sex as if they really existed in America, as indeed he had seen them exist in Indiana when he was a boy. But he was also damaged by the fact that he did not measure up to any of the current popular concepts of a literary person of his day. . . . It was . . . expected of Hoosiers that they write uplifting stories about just plain folks or romantic tales of never-never lands, and Dreiser did neither."[32] The fact was that he simply could not.

Not only poverty separated Dreiser from polite society; his ethnicity also placed him outside the pale. Prior to *Sister Carrie* the literary world had been peopled by insiders—Anglo-Saxon, Protestant, educated. Dreiser, the son of German immigrants, did not so much lack respect for conventional society as he lacked firsthand experience of it. He was awkward, unsophisticated, and brash. Alfred Kazin called him, not entirely unkindly, "that Indiana barbarian,"[33] and Parrington referred to him as "a huge figure of ungainly proportions. . . . He tramps across fields straight to his objective, messing sadly the neat little beds of American convention, peering into the secret places."[34]

Much has been made of what Philip Gerber in *Theodore Dreiser Revisited* referred to as the "revolutionary subtext of all of Dreiser's novels."[35] But Dreiser was not a revolutionary, social or literary, so much as he simply wrote about the world as he saw it around him. Editor John Lydenberg writes in *Dreiser: A Collection of Critical Essays* that Dreiser was an unwitting revolutionary, that "simply because he looked at the world about him with untrained uncultured eyes and insisted on being himself, he brought a revolution to American literature."[36] Lydenberg also suggests that "the power of [Dreiser's] novels lies precisely in the fact that they were not illustrations of any political ideas or social theories."[37]

Ronald Weber views Dreiser more regionally than do other literary historians. "What is remarkable about Dreiser, seen in a regionalist light, is indeed the absence from his fiction of much of the familiar Midwestern literary landscape. There is in his imaginative work no suggestion of a garden myth to affirm or deny, no stories of rural returns punctuated with ambivalent feelings, no current of resistance to a Midwest of folk charm or grim futility. *That* Midwest simply holds no place in his imagination; it is not rejected so much as it simply does not exist."[38] It was not that Dreiser set out to smash any literary icons; he simply had no access to what Weber called "the world on the other side of the iron fences."[39]

Rather than a revolutionary subtext, there is an innocence and childlike credulity in Dreiser's fiction. Lydenberg suggested, as have others, that Dreiser "saw a world made up of the strong and the weak instead of the good and the bad,"[40] and it was this very inability to distinguish moral certainties that disturbed the reading public most about the naturalists.

For Dreiser the vagaries of individual fortunes were mysterious, governed not by human actions and logical consequences but by chance and the impersonal forces of nature. In Lydenberg's collection, H. L. Mencken contends that "this complete rejection of ethical plan and purpose, this manifestation of . . . moral innocence, is what brought up the guardians of the national tradition at the gallop, and created the Dreiser bugaboo of today. All the rubber-stamp formulae of American fiction were thrown overboard in these earlier books . . . one could find in them no orderly chain of causes and effects, of rewards and punishments; they represented life as a phenomenon at once terrible and unintelligible, like a stroke of lightning."[41]

The image of lightning appears again in Weber's discussion of Dreiser and the beginnings of the naturalist movement in America. "When the lightning rod of that development arrived in the unlikely person of Theodore Dreiser, he would come, with fine irony, from Indiana, though from an underworld of poverty far removed from the comfortable towns of the historical novelists or the equally comfortable literary Indianapolis of Tarkington and Riley. And neither Howells nor Garland, let alone his fellow Indiana writers, would immediately recognize his startling presence among them."[42]

Whether the literary community recognized and simply chose to ignore him is unclear. Later generations, with some exceptions, continued to snub Dreiser. In his otherwise comprehensive study of Indiana literature, published in 1962, Arthur Shumaker dismissed Dreiser with a sentence. "Very reluctantly David Graham Phillips and Theodore Dreiser have been excluded because of insufficient residence and Indiana influence in their works."[43] More recent Indiana historians have included, even embraced, Dreiser, perhaps recognizing in him the state's one literary lion.

Dreiser's shunning may have been due to the misconception that he rejected Indiana in some way. While he did make an occasional disparaging remark about the rural Midwest, considering his miserable childhood, he was surprisingly nostalgic when he wrote *A Hoosier Holiday*, a lengthy account of a car trip with a friend to revisit the Indiana of his youth. "How good it all tasted after New York! And what a spell it cast. I can scarcely make you understand, I fear. Indiana is a world all unto itself. . . . The air felt

*Pen and ink of Theodore Dreiser, the Indiana-born author who helped change
literary history with his novel* Sister Carrie.

different—the sky and trees and streets here were sweeter. . . .
The intervening years frizzled away and once more I saw myself
quite clearly in this region, with the ideas and moods of my youth
still dominant. I was a 'kid' again, and these streets and stores

were as familiar to me as though I had lived in them all my life."[44] Still, he recalled of Terre Haute that "somewhere there was a small house . . . [that] remains the apotheosis of earthly gloom to me even now."[45]

Likely, this contradiction can be attributed to the natural nostalgia of maturity and middle age and the fact that the intervening years had opened the mysterious world of material and social success to Dreiser. Still, in recalling the early days, he could well remember that "the fact that the world [in part] was busy about feasts and pleasures, that there were drawingrooms lighted for receptions, diningrooms for dinner, ballrooms for dancing, and that I was nowhere included, was an aching thorn. I used to stroll about where theatres were just receiving their influx of evening patrons or where some function of note was being held, and stare with avid eyes at the preparations. I felt lone and lorn. A rather weak and profitless tendency, say you? Quite so; I admit it. It interests me now quite as much as it possibly could you. I am now writing of myself not as I am, but as I was."[46]

The Dreiser that *was* can be found readily enough in four novels set, at least in part, in various places in the Midwest, which reflect Dreiser's early childhood in Indiana. The novels, *Sister Carrie*, *Jennie Gerhardt*, *The "Genius,"* and *An American Tragedy*, are considered to be the most autobiographical of Dreiser's works of fiction and are imprinted with Dreiser's obsessive fear of poverty. In *Dawn* Dreiser wrote that "for years, even so late as my thirty-fifth or fortieth year, the approach of winter invariably filled me with an indefinable and highly oppressive dread."[47] This very dread is what compels Carrie Meeber to accept twenty dollars from a prosperous admirer for winter clothing. From there it is a short step to accepting a room and the comparative security of the role of mistress.

Sister Carrie is the story of a naive, rural midwestern girl who goes to Chicago to seek her fortune. Driven by economic necessity to accept the support of various gentlemen, she eventually finds success and financial independence as an actress, though she never finds contentment. Through Carrie's eyes the reader sees Chicago quite vividly as Dreiser saw it as a newly independent, young man. She portrays not only his wide-eyed fascination with the city, but also his sense of desperation and isolation.

Carrie also, like Jennie Gerhardt and Roberta Alden in *An American Tragedy*, represents an amalgam of several of Dreiser's sisters who endured the stigmas of illegitimacies and associations with elderly "patrons." Dreiser poured his personal rage over the social and economic conditions that victimized young working-class women into *Sister Carrie*. In *The "Genius"* he continued to press the conviction that "life was somehow bigger and subtler and darker than any given theory or order of living. It might well be worth while for a man or woman to be honest and moral within a given condition or quality of society, but it did not matter at all in the ultimate substance and composition of the universe."[48] In *Dawn* he challenged the reader to "measure the thinness of literature and of moral dogma and religious control by your own observations and experiences. Look back over your own life and see!"[49] So it is that Carrie and Jennie cannot really be condemned, in Dreiser's opinion, for the choices they have been compelled by circumstances to make.

Jennie Gerhardt is the most revelatory of Dreiser's novels that touch on the grim circumstances of his youth and the idiosyncrasies of his parents and siblings. *The "Genius"* is the novel in which Dreiser, through character Eugene Witla, explores most fully his own profligate sexuality and his estimation of himself as an artist. "They might reject him," Witla muses regarding his own critics. "If so that would merely prove that they did not recognize a radical departure from accepted methods and subject matter as art."[50]

Witla is a painter, but he clearly represents Dreiser's career as a writer. A fictional review of Witla's work taken from the novel could almost have served as an enlightened review of Dreiser's own work. "A new painter . . . has an oil . . . which for directness, virility, sympathy, faithfulness to detail and what for want of a better term we may call totality of spirit, is quite the best thing in the exhibition. It looks rather out of place surrounded by the weak and spindling interpretations of scenery and water which so readily find a place in the exhibition of the Academy, but it is none the weaker for that. The artist has a new, crude, raw and almost rough method, but his picture seems to say quite clearly what he sees and feels."[51]

It is in *An American Tragedy* that Dreiser's most fundamental social and literary concerns are revealed—an inordinate preoccupation with class and social standing and an almost puerile fascination with wealth, power, and sex. *An American Tragedy* is the story of Clyde Griffiths, a young man so consumed by his lust for wealth and social position that he plans the murder of the girl he has seduced. Roberta Alden becomes pregnant, and she manages to force Clyde to assume some measure of responsibility for her situation. Meanwhile, however, Clyde has become interested in a society girl and is convinced that Roberta is trying to trap him. Roberta drowns in a boating "accident," but Clyde is so bereft of a sense of moral responsibility and of empathy that he goes to the electric chair uncertain, himself, whether he is actually guilty of her death.

An American Tragedy is the culmination of the unflinching examination of the reality of life in the American city that Dreiser began with *Sister Carrie*. In his contribution to *Critical Essays on Theodore Dreiser*, Robert Penn Warren stated that Clyde's "'tragedy' is that of namelessness, and this is one aspect of its being an American tragedy, the story of the individual without identity, whose responsible self has been absorbed by the great machine of modern industrial secularized society, and reduced to a cog, a cipher, an abstraction."[52] Early in the novel while Clyde is fleeing the scene of a previous tragic "accident" he instinctively flees *into* the city, where he can disappear. Similarly Carrie and Jennie found in the anonymity of the city a freedom from social conventions and thereby from a measure of culpability. In *The American City Novel* Gelfant states that "in exploring the inner emptiness of city life, [Dreiser] gave an early and significant expression to the sense of loss and uncertainty that seems to be the common subjective experience treated in modern literature."[53]

David Graham Phillips was contemporary with Dreiser and Tarkington. Phillips was born in 1867 in Madison, Indiana,

David Graham Phillips as a young reporter. Known principally as a muckraker, he was a prolific novelist before his career was cut short by his murder in 1911.

attended Indiana Asbury (now DePauw University), graduated from Princeton, and worked for several Cincinnati and New York newspapers. He was at the top of his profession when, in 1901, he published his first novel, *The Great God Success*.

Dozens of novels followed. Several were set in Indiana—St. X. in the case of *The Cost* and *The Second Generation*, and Remsen City in the case of *The Plum Tree* and *The Conflict*. All are reform novels that treat the subjects of political corruption, big business monopoly, and exploitation of the working class. The central character in both *The Cost* and *The Plum Tree* is Senator Hampden Scarborough, a fictionalized Albert J. Beveridge, who was a close friend and former college roommate of Phillips.

Just as Dreiser's name became synonymous with the naturalist movement, Phillips's name was inextricably linked with the muckrakers. Indeed, while he achieved only a passing notoriety for his fiction, Phillips is still remembered for an explosive series of articles in 1906 called "The Treason of the Senate," which contributed significantly to election reform and represented the pinnacle of exposé journalism.

While the muckrakers and the naturalists addressed many of the same issues, they did so from markedly different perspectives. Phillips and Dreiser knew each other; they were both at the *New York World* at the same time. While they both subscribed to a social Darwinism that pitted the strong against the weak and rendered standard moral codes untenable, their agendas were as unlike as their backgrounds had been. Phillips, who had come from a prosperous and happy family, wrote reform novels that preached, often too overtly, a political ideal or sought a political solution to social ills. Where Phillips sought to effect social change, Dreiser sought simply to report social conditions as he saw them. For Dreiser there were no solutions for society at large. There were only temporary compensations that could be arrived at on an individual basis, compensations that proved, too often, to be inadequate.

For Phillips the mark of the machine was to be seen not only in the effects of industrialization, the machine age, on the working classes, but also in the tyranny of machine politics powered by Wall Street. For Dreiser the "machine" was simply the workings of a mechanical universe without an absolute moral law. Where Phillips had nothing but contempt for the plutocracy, Dreiser aspired to it.

Phillips's career was cut short by his murder in 1911 in Gramercy Park at the hands of a deluded reader who thought Phillips had disparaged his family in one of the novels. Unfortunately, it was with the last novel, *Susan Lenox, Her Fall and Rise*, a massive two-volume masterpiece of feminist literature, published posthumously in 1917, that Phillips's potential as a novelist can be seen. There are striking similarities between *Susan Lenox* and *Sister Carrie*. Both novels use the vehicle of the theater profession to explore false social values. Both Susan and Carrie, as actresses, hide behind costumes and numerous roles in a society that judges people solely by fashion, and in which women's roles are no longer clearly defined. Both women have left behind places that represent traditional values and sought the opportunities and anonymity of the city, an anonymity that frees them from social conventions. Both books are brutal stories of survival. In *Susan Lenox* a marginal character could speak to both Susan and Carrie Meeber when he predicts, "you'll see that you were right at first when you thought only the strong could afford to do right. And you'll see that you were right in the second stage when you thought only the strong could afford to do wrong. For you'll have learned that only the strong can afford to act at all, and that they can do right or wrong as they please *because they are strong.*"[54]

Today Dreiser is considered to be a giant of American literature, while Phillips and Tarkington remain footnotes, quite literally, in most literary histories. In ignoring Dreiser and elevating Tarkington, previous generations of Hoosiers may well have done their state a disservice. The provincial attitude that persisted in its attachment to romanticism and moral messages in literature may have kept Indiana from entering the age of naturalism and, thus, the modern era, and limited its literary fame to one brief shining moment at the turn of the century.

Kazin concludes that "our modern literature was rooted in those dark and still little-understood years of the 1880s and 1890s when all America stood suddenly, as it were, between one society and another, one moral order and another, and the sense of impending change became almost oppressive in its vividness. . . . But above all was it rooted in the need to learn what the reality of life was in the modern era."[55]

It was not that Tarkington was so much less a realist than was Dreiser; his reality simply differed radically from Dreiser's. For Tarkington, the world of Alice Adams was the real world, just as Carrie Meeber's world was Dreiser's. Tarkington sought, in his own gentlemanly way, to bridge the widening gulf between the old and new world orders. Dreiser simply came along and burned the bridge behind him, leaving Indiana on the other side.

CHAPTER FIVE

"So Saturate with Earth"

Rural and Farm Fiction between the Wars

There were two distinct periods in which what could be termed rural or agrarian fiction rose to a level of some prominence in American literature. The first, characterized principally by rusticity of setting and an attempt at authentic vernacular, was really part of the local-color movement and early attempts at realism. While local-color authors, such as Edward Eggleston, introduced farm characters and settings, the realities of farm life and the true nature of the farm "type," as opposed to caricature, had not been addressed significantly in American literature. Farm life was not considered, by the eastern literary establishment, to be worthy of literary exploration. Ruth Suckow, writing in the *English Journal* in March 1932, used the term "colonial hang-over" to describe the literary conventions of the time that "still darkens, and to some extent blights, all creative art in this country."[1]

Though the ideal of the yeoman farmer, as Henry Nash Smith first delineated it, was a commonly held cultural myth of the early nineteenth century, the literary conventions of the time were strongly marked by class, and according to Smith, members of the lower class, which farmers as laborers were considered to be, figured in early-nineteenth-century novels only in "subordinate roles."[2] Subordinate roles could in fact be a euphemism for what Wilson O. Clough in *The Necessary Earth: Nature and Solitude in American Literature* suggests was, all too often, the role of "clown, slave, serf, oaf . . . , automatically barred from the concerns of high literature."[3]

It was what Smith called this "incongruity between literary convention and the materials of western life"[4] that gave the local-color movement its impetus and its significance. The contribution of writers such as Edward Eggleston was not that their rural characters deviated significantly from qualities of boorishness, it was that rural characters figured prominently as central characters at all in dramas about ordinary people in ordinary places. In fact Eggleston, to some extent, and particularly other local colorists such as E. W. Howe and Joseph Kirkland, painted quite unflattering, oftentimes humorous portraits of downright rubelike characters.

Smith's incongruities were not entirely the fault of the eastern establishment. Midwestern readers contributed to the perpetuation of sentimental scenarios peopled with genteel characters, perhaps because rural settings and subjects were too immediate and ordinary to be considered the stuff of fiction. The average reader wanted to be transported to another time and place in his or her rare hours for leisure reading, not reminded of the tedious routines and familiar vistas of his or her own daily existence.

Though farm fiction had its antecedents before the turn of the century, it did not really begin to blossom until well into the twentieth century with what Ronald Weber perceives as the first acute awareness of "the loss of a natural pastoral life" and yearnings for "rural returns touched with feelings of nostalgia."[5] This awareness was driven in large part by observation of the effects of industrialization and urbanization, disillusionment following World War I, and later by the economic impact of the depression. Pining for a return to a simple, rural existence was in vogue in the 1920s and 1930s, and farm fiction served as a palliative. Predictably, this literature took several forms. Lesser authors capitalized on the nostalgia, returning to the myth of the yeoman farmer and glorifying his lifestyle, pandering to the romantic vein that still satisfied large numbers of readers. Others experimented with social criticism, stressing the plight of the farmer in harsh economic times and the forces that were changing the face of farming forever, what Roy W. Meyer, in *The Middle Western Farm Novel in the Twentieth Century*, called "the strident regionalism of the early

1920's."[6] A third, and more important, style of farm literature rode the rising tide of realism, attempting to capture what Weber calls "plain people in a plain environment living plain lives."[7] Leonard Lutwack notes that in American literature the "anti-pastoral note . . . [had been] a more dominant strain than the pastoral,"[8] and that "it was not until the latter part of the nineteenth century, with the new power acquired by the novel through realism, that literature could do justice to the sad state of the pastoral ideal in America."[9]

What began as a mild interest in that ideal became a virtual publishing frenzy in the 1920s and 1930s. "By 1925 the novels that drew from this new fruitful field were being recognized as constituting a definite school of American fiction, characterized by material rather than by method," wrote Caroline B. Sherman in the January 1938 issue of *Agricultural History*.[10] A *New York Times Book Review* feature in 1925 remarked on "the large public who are intrigued by novels of farm life,"[11] and another in 1930 pronounced that "any piece of fiction which evokes the prairie and farm life with competent realism is certain of a reading in these days when many a harried city dweller turns a nostalgic eye toward the disappearing country life of his youth."[12]

This phenomenon was not received enthusiastically by all observers. What one critic viewed as a positive "fidelity to farm life and values,"[13] another viewed as "a stupendous monotony." In a July 1924 article in *The Forum* the latter contended that "thanks to the new school of novelists we are all pretty thoroughly versed in the secret yearnings and complexes of the average farmer's wife, to say nothing of the average hired girl." He goes on to quip that, "A professional book-reviewer nowadays feels qualified to go out and run any farm in Iowa."[14]

This glib assessment belies the most critical credential for authentic farm fiction according to Meyer. In his analysis, Meyer distinguishes between fiction "which deals [only] incidentally and peripherally with farm life,"[15] usually authored by nonfarmers, and the real thing, which he contends is "the product of writers whose knowledge of rural life is sound and extensive, [and which] will reproduce with great fidelity the daily and seasonal tasks of the farmer and his family, their amusements and social activities, and the sights and sounds, and smells of the physical environment in which they live."[16]

Presumably this intimacy with the farm as a distinct narrative place could be realized only from personal and direct experience. Though Meyer more than acknowledges the legacy of Eggleston, who, though he had some experience with farm life was not really a farmer, and mentions Maurice Thompson's *Hoosier Mosaics* briefly in passing, the only Indiana literature he raises up as an example of authentic farm fiction is the work of LeRoy Oliver MacLeod.

MacLeod was born in Anderson, Indiana, in 1893. He grew up on a farm not far from Crawfordsville and spent several years farming there after graduating from DePauw University in 1915, before moving on to careers in journalism and advertising. His first published work was a collection of poetry related to rural life published in 1929. In 1931 he published the first of three novels set in the Wabash valley, *Three Steeples: A Tragedy of Earth*. It was MacLeod's first novel and his weakest, but it did demonstrate potential to a handful of local critics. Perhaps what makes it less artistically compelling than the two later novels, *The Years of Peace* and *The Crowded Hill*, published in 1932 and 1934 respectively, is not so much the immaturity of style, but rather the fact that it qualifies as one of those "incidental" farm novels. Though its principal characters are a farm boy and the other residents of an Indiana farming community, it is not really *about* farm life and so perhaps it lacks what Meyer calls the "documentary vividness"[17] of the later novels. By "documentary" Meyer did not mean to suggest that MacLeod's style was journalistic, though he does acknowledge a certain "restrained and sometimes under-written treatment of emotion"[18] in the later two novels.

Meyer, while he did not consider MacLeod's novels to be great literature, did consider them to be "fiction of considerable distinction."[19] MacLeod's novels have been criticized for their lack of plot. And while it is true that not much happens in them, and that what does happen happens slowly, it also is true that one of the functions of farm fiction, and certainly one of MacLeod's objectives, was to reflect, as accurately as possible, what William Dean Howells called "the same days and weeks of horrible dullness," which filled the average person's everyday life.[20] If this depiction was painful, so much the better. Monotony, sometimes suffocating, sometimes restorative, was part and parcel of the farm lifestyle. Much earlier than MacLeod or any of the new breed of farm novelists, Eggleston had made it apparent in *The Graysons* that "a farm-house on the edge of an unsettled prairie is a dull place, where all things have a monotonous, diurnal revolution and a larger annual repetition."[21]

The "cycle of planting, harvesting, and plowing is repeated again and again"[22] in *The Years of Peace*, just as on any working farm. But MacLeod, in the very routine of his characters' lives, managed to transcend the bucolic images of farm life heretofore popular and to convey instead something of the human drama of ordinary lives. He accomplishes this because the habitual behaviors of the characters are suffused with emotional content, both creative and destructive. Meyer introduces MacLeod in his chapter entitled "The Farm Novelist as Psychologist," and the novels are profoundly psychological as they explore the interior lives and the wounded marriage of Tyler and Evaline Peck.

Tyler and Evaline are introspective characters, aware of their own motivations without being implausibly cerebral. Tyler, particularly, is a complex character. Flawed and faithless though he is, he continually redeems himself by small acts of generosity, compassion, and humility. He can be exquisitely charming or utterly boorish. He is as realistic and multidimensional a character as any in Indiana literature.

While Tyler is the more compelling personality, the reader gains equal insight into Evaline's character. This circumstance reflected a growing literary trend. Meyer noted that realism precipitated a vogue in psychological domestic novels that addressed women's roles and the everyday realities of marriage, and that the farm, by its very nature, seemed to have been a particularly conducive setting. Isolation, monotony, economic pressures, and conservatism regarding traditional roles all conspired against the average farmwife. Lutwack noted in *The Role of Place in Literature* that "when chores cannot be lightened in some way, the farm becomes a burden and the farmhouse a place of terrible fears and hopeless alienation between man and woman."[23]

Evaline Peck is sometimes victimized by all of these circumstances, but she is not a traditional victim. She carries, if not accepts, her full share of responsibility for the marital discord in her household. To her husband Evaline seemed "so full of Sabbath."[24] By rebuffing his every gesture of intimacy and by lacking all humor or sense of adventure, she sabotages, day by day, her own vision of what marriage could be. When he slips an arm under her head in bed she complains that he is pulling her hair. Returning to the house one evening Tyler almost forgets to bring Evvie a "punkin" as he had promised and ends up bringing too many by way of compensation. "One would have been enough," Evaline scolds. Utterly deflated, Tyler silently watches her "washing the cheeks of the great brown vegetable as if it were a child's face, or its bottom."[25]

And so their introspection causes their countless small actions to resonate with meaning. Carter Harrison writing in the *Indianapolis News* in 1934 referred to "the tremendous trifles of the lives of the Pecks." While his praise of the novel is effusive, he was insightful in his opinion that "here . . . is a book which plumbs so gently and deeply the life of the Pecks that an Indiana farm becomes the cosmos and the reader wiser."[26]

The routine clearing and burning of a thicket in *The Crowded Hill* is illuminated by Tyler's memories of a meaningless assignation in the very place with Evvie's hired girl. MacLeod focuses on the details of the work and deftly underplays the memories of the sexual encounter, making of it almost a subtext, because that is what it was in Tyler's life. Tyler's contemplation of the transgression causes him some discomfort as he works, but it is as brief and ultimately uninspiring as the event itself.

Meyer's three criteria for authentic farm fiction are an accurate portrayal of the daily life and physical environment associated with a working farm, attention to accurate language or dialect, and the reflection of attitudes or a belief system typical of farm people. He felt the latter to include "conservatism, individualism, anti-intellectualism, hostility to the town, and a type of primitivism."[27] In *On Native Grounds* Alfred Kazin gave the concept a more rural tone by calling it "detestation of the high-falutin'."[28]

All Meyer's criteria are exhibited in MacLeod's two farm novels. Daily life and physical environment, particularly, are captured with astonishing clarity in vivid sensory images—"the smell of dust in which the sheep had lain,"[29] or "the flatted clank of a sheep bell."[30] In the novels "a week is a pattern for a month in the Wabash Valley, a month for a year, a year for a lifetime." MacLeod reenforces this theme with the following passage.

> In late April and May Tyler planted corn. In June he began cultivating with the double-shovel, down one side of a row and up the other. Then the hay had to be cut and stacked or stowed in the mow. July finished the hay and cut the wheat, the oats. But the cultivation went on among the corn-rows till the swords of the blades hung over him. In August the small grain was threshed and the fences mended. In September the fall plowing started, wheat was sowed in the corn, the fruit picked. . . . In October the shucking began, the fodder-cutting. The hickory-nuts, walnuts, butternuts, hazelnuts, and punkins were gathered. By the end of November, with good luck, the corn harvest was finished. In the snowy months the stock were tended, wood cut, rails split. In late February or early March the sugar-trees were tapped and the syrup made. In late March the oats and clover were sowed and the plow set to turning new furrows. By the last of April the clock of the year was round to planting time again.[31]

The Years of Peace is, in fact, divided into two sections that are called simply "Plowing" and "Planting." When Tyler was plowing "the man saw no higher than the wooden beam of the plow, the dirt curling aside, the singletrees swayed by the traces, the paired hocks passing each other like scissor-blades, the limp tails blowing . . . he might have been merely another beast, another implement, so completely does a laborer of the earth seem a thing of the earth."[32] Similarly, Carl, the Pecks' oldest boy, works all day planting corn and is still "dropping corn in his dreams."[33]

The suffocating sense of sameness and entrapment is in large part a function of Tyler's attitude, and it competes in his consciousness with a genuine appreciation for the peaceful community in which he lives and his good fortune, for which he needs to remind himself to be thankful. "Life stretched before him sublime and wonderful, a new and inexhaustible field given him as a gift, yet every year to be won like the spoils of a great war, as he plowed it afresh and planted again."[34]

Ironically, the theme of war or conflict is reflected on multiple levels in this novel titled *The Years of Peace*. While there is peace in the valley following Appomattox, the farmer battles daily against nature, and there is no peace in the Peck household.

In addition, MacLeod begins most of his chapters with accounts of conflicts throughout the world that impact only tangentially life in the Wabash valley, if at all. The Civil War, which has just ended at the beginning of the novel, has scarcely touched Indiana. The most conflict seen in Tyler's household as a result of the war has been caused by his southern sympathies. The early chapters of the book are marked by references to the conflict, "the first day" referring to the first day after Appomattox. But the second day, third day, and so on soon devolve into "a cloudy day at the very last of June," and "a cold day in January," days distinguished only by season and weather, rather than by human events. On a day in October "the horizon has closed in. If one stands among the trees the trees are infinite. If one stands in the corn the world is forested with corn. The third-dimensional horizon of the sky has also closed in, so that the sun is equally imaginary with the moon and stars, and the time might be morning or afternoon. How can one believe that in Sumatra, where night is, a war is?"[35]

War imagery reflects Tyler's struggles to subdue nature and on the day in 1870 in which "some sixteen thousand Germans and French were mowed down in the Battle of Worth. . . . In the afternoon Tyler attacked with his scythe the ironweed army on the way to the big road—bending, swaying, jerking in a drunkenness of slaughter."[36] Thus Tyler Peck continues in the long tradition of farmers who seek to be "the final victors in the battle against Nature, completing the process that hunters . . . and squatters had begun," as Ray Allen Billington expressed the impulse in *Land of Savagery, Land of Promise: The European Image of the American Frontier in the Nineteenth Century*.[37]

The theme of conflict, represented in macrocosm by global conflicts, is reflected in microcosm by the Pecks' marriage. While there is peace in the valley, there is only the appearance of peace in the Peck household, and only discord in the hearts and minds of the Pecks themselves. Tyler in particular is not at peace, finding himself in a loveless marriage and trapped in an occupation for which he has even less passion. He is riddled by guilt about his numerous indiscretions and conflicted about his seven children, perceiving them as so many encumbrances, rendering his adolescent spirit ever more earthbound. "Each was another chain forged out of her body to bind him."[38]

Tyler's better nature strives to emulate his esteemed Uncle Lafe, a model of respectability, but he never quite measures up in his own mind, and he loses the battle with his sexual appetites at every turn. Tyler is quick to blame Evaline and various impersonal forces, yet he is fully cognizant of his shortcomings and accepts the consequences of his own decisions. It is the latter quality that makes him the sympathetic and multifaceted character that he is and allows the reader to identify with him in spite of his faults. He is not the "honest husbandman" immune to the temptations and sins of regular men. Neither is he an amoral, depersonalized figure tumbling helplessly in the tide of naturalism.

The hostility between townsfolk and farm folk, one of Meyer's farm novel criteria, is less developed. On one level the two opposing camps merely reflect the basic human need to recognize, if not manufacture, social group distinctions. Since the beginnings of American literature, authors have pitted the frontiersman against the farmer, the farm folk against the townsfolk, the small town against the big city. But the local-color movement in the Midwest seems to have reflected a more fundamental and formative self-consciousness about social position vis-à-vis eastern sensibilities. Underlying the heartfelt contempt of rural Americans for "city-ites" was, undeniably, a profound inferiority complex. Without the narrative value of this sensitivity, a true regional literature might not have developed to the degree that it did.

Another component of the rivalry was a genuine conviction that "fresh air and hard physical work exert a sanative influence on human beings." Meyer refers to this as the "simple, biological level" of a theory of rural eminence. "At other times," he continued, "it approaches a mystical concept of the essential unity of man with nature, a unity spiritual as well as physical."[39]

MacLeod's last book, *The Crowded Hill*, continues the lives of the Pecks as they move into the big house, which they have inherited after Uncle Lafe's death, and which they must share with his embittered widow and her daughter. While this sequel is less about farming and more about politics, it continues the themes of multileveled conflict and of the seclusion and isolation of the Pecks. Again the time is marked by seasonal chores and concerns. "Day by day Evaline's diary followed the calendar toward August. Many important things were set down, but no mention of the Russians crossing the Danube, no mention of the awful railroad strikes in this country."[40] Even the county seat and its problems—"the low prices, the scarce money, the mortgage foreclosures, the insecurity of banks, . . . charity . . . increasing its demands upon the county and municipal funds"[41]—seem far away and fundamentally unimportant. Instead, Tyler hears "the drift of the day in the clock's tick, and the tea kettle's whine and the women's voices saying nothing."[42]

In *The Crowded Hill* the town versus country conflict is more pronounced than in the former novel, because Tyler dabbles in local politics and therefore must step out into the world and away from the solitariness and shelter of the farm. It is then that he encounters and tries to endure the condescension of townsfolk, as on one morning in town when Tyler is greeted by a group of men who need his support on a political issue. In greeting him the judge remarks on the "wonderful rain for the corn." Tyler agrees as he grips "the soft hand," while thinking to himself: "These patronizing townsmen!—a lot they cared whether the corn got rain or not!"[43]

Old Aaron, a neighbor of the Pecks, who had virtually disowned his two daughters for moving to St. Louis and Louisville, refers to them as "city-ites" and says to Tyler, "I'd like to catch every last one of them there nicey nicey women with their snoots in the air and make 'em kneel down in a *nice, juicy* cowlot in fly time and milk the greenest-tailed cows I could lay hands on—and *then* see how their noses looked. And their men folks—I'd like to find me a *nice, sour* old hog waller, oh 'bout belly-button deep or such a matter, and sock 'em down in it till the top o' the loblolly just sorta tickled the hairs o' their noses. Then when they'd had a good big whiff I'd reach me out a fence rail and press down on 'em gentle like—an see how sweet they looked when they come up."[44]

The unromantic realities of rural life, of bodily functions, sexuality, and death are depicted repeatedly throughout MacLeod's novels, whether picturesquely as in "yellow butterflies swarming up from the droppings in the road,"[45] or in graphic details of the laying out of a dead neighbor or the killing of a troublesome cat. MacLeod's gift for eliciting discomfort through detail is at its most pronounced, however, in his depictions of the three most odious seasonal chores—hay harvesting, hoeing corn, and shucking corn. "Shucking corn in the still frosty fall—the cobwebs across your face; the chaff of brittle blades and tassels in your eyes; tickle grass inching up inside your trouser legs; sometimes rain, sleet, snow making the shucks stubborn and cracking your hands open with sores—the straining vigilance for the next ear to be stooped for or reached for in a second—a whole wagon-load to be filled, one ear at a time, whack, thump on the bang board!—three heaping loads from lanterns out to lanterns lit, whole fields before winter—and the muzzled team for company."[46]

For all its rural ambiance and its identity as an agricultural state, as well as a literary one, Indiana has produced surprisingly few farm novelists that meet Meyer's criteria, and none of any great stature. It has not produced the likes of Nebraska's Willa Cather, for example, for whom the rural setting is more than integral to her stories; it is virtually the story itself.

If, however, one expands the genre to include pastoral literature, with what Simon Schama would call its arcadian qualities,

Formal portrait of Gene Stratton-Porter as a young woman.

including an awareness of and appreciation for land and its power to shape, and sometimes restore human lives, then Indiana has some notable voices.[47]

Gene Stratton-Porter was not only one of the most prolific and popular writers of the golden age, but also an amateur naturalist and photographer at a time when nature was enjoying unprecedented national attention and popularity. She started publishing in outdoor magazines, her articles often sounding alarms that eventually put her in the forefront of a nationwide conservation movement. Biographer Judith Reick Long called her one of two contemporaneous "American giants . . . who sought to reshape the national perspective,"[48] the other being Theodore Roosevelt. Long notes that by 1920 Stratton-Porter's name was "a household word around the globe,"[49] and indeed Stratton-Porter was one of the best-selling authors of her time. She was also the author of a popular column in *McCall's* magazine that did much to familiarize the average reader with her positions and stimulate interest in her books.

Stratton-Porter's novels were unapologetically bucolic and so wholesome and romantic that they have been dismissed wholesale by critics. Stratton-Porter believed strongly that literature could and should uplift and ennoble as well as educate and entertain the reader. Whether her novels were about the timber industry, as was *Freckles*, the collecting of moth specimens as was *A Girl of the Limberlost*, or the cultivation and harvesting of medicinal herbs and roots as in *The Harvester*, Stratton-Porter wrote most frequently of heroes and heroines whose livelihood and spiritual well-being were intimately connected to the land and in conflict with the various forces that would exploit and destroy it.

Stratton-Porter was a farm girl until her father abandoned farming in the Panic of 1873 and moved his family to the town of Wabash, Indiana, where she lived until she married in her early twenties. Stratton-Porter was the youngest of twelve children, and Long suggests that the stresses of such a large family in tough economic times, particularly after the death of the mother, contributed to a somewhat dysfunctional family dynamic that Stratton-Porter denied in later life. Indeed, farms do not fare very well as settings in her novels. As contrasted with the woods, in particular, farms are characterized by dirt, despair, and poverty, as, for example, in *A Girl of the Limberlost* or *A Daughter of the Land*. In both instances the farm is a place from which to escape and the woods is a sanctuary. In *A Daughter of the Land* Kate flees to the woods where she "sat on a log, a most unusual occurrence for her, for she was familiar only with bare, hot houses, furnished with meager necessities; reeking stables, barnyards and vegetable gardens. She knew less of the woods than the average city girl; but there was a soothing wind, a sweet perfume, a calming silence that quieted her tense mood and enabled her to think clearly."[50]

In most of the author's Indiana novels a love interest or other significant character must be convinced of the value of a rural life. In the case of *A Girl of the Limberlost* it is the heroine herself, and her embittered mother, who ultimately find, or perhaps fashion happiness right in their own backyard.

Arthur Shumaker called Stratton-Porter the best known of the popular Indiana authors though he also characterized her as "a popular novelist only, a representative of the back-to-nature movement . . . but of practically no real literary value to the mature reader."[51] With this assessment Shumaker touched on an aspect of agrarian fiction that can be applied equally to many farm novels, and goes far in explaining their appeal. "The truth is," Shumaker wrote, "that her typical writings have always appealed essentially to the simple-minded . . . [who derive] a therapeutic effect from their imaginative return to nature and the idyllic simple life."[52] While it may be excessive to call Stratton-Porter's readers unsophisticated, it is true that the gentle nostalgia and Old-World values that she promoted did (and does) account for most, if not all of her appeal.

Whether or not her readers were unsophisticated, Stratton-Porter took every opportunity to insist that she herself was not. "It rather frets me to be mistaken for a poor fool who does not even know that evil exists in the world. I do, truly!" she wrote in an article in the August 1919 issue of *American Magazine*. "I merely refuse to discuss it intimately on the pages of a work which I especially design to interest people in the happiness and health to be

Limberlost Cabin in Geneva, Indiana, first home of Gene Stratton-Porter as a married woman.

Wildflower Woods near Rome City, Indiana. Gene Stratton-Porter built this home in 1914. Like Limberlost Cabin, it remains a state historic site.

found afield."[53] Long claims that Stratton-Porter's first novels simply catered to "the current editorial and public preference for a
romance set in a mythical kingdom, a craze for stories about roy-
alty that had reached epidemic proportions."[54] According to Long,
the beginnings of her career serendipitously coincided with the
newly established Doubleday, Page and Company that had already
begun to publish "a stream of well-advertised nature books, both
fiction and nonfiction. By October 1904, when *Freckles* was
released," Long asserts, "the reading public was avidly receptive
to Doubleday's nature lore push."[55]

Most of Stratton-Porter's fiction was, if not literally autobiographical, heavily influenced by and reflective of her life in rural
Indiana. *Laddie* is perhaps the most directly autobiographical of
her novels. The hero was based on her older brother Leander,
whom she actually called Laddie. The character of the harvester
in the book of the same name is patterned after her father, though
in real life it was actually her mother who sent Stratton-Porter to
the woods as a young girl to gather materials for concocting her
homemade medicines. Both *Laddie* and *A Girl of the Limberlost*
relate true stories of Stratton-Porter's childhood experiences, particularly with school and in various social situations. Both are
marginally farm stories. A story more deserving of the label farm
fiction is the overlooked but interesting novel entitled *A Daughter
of the Land*. While the heroine of this novel does not directly
reflect Stratton-Porter's childhood experiences, the depiction of
farm life and its impact on a young woman's psyche are detailed
and authentic. In the story Kate is the youngest of sixteen children and is a virtual slave on her parents' farm. "As usual, she had
left her bed at four o'clock; for seven hours she had cooked,
washed dishes, made beds, swept, dusted, milked, churned, following the usual routine of a big family in the country."[56] Kate
knows that only her brothers will inherit pieces of her father's vast
holdings. When she runs away to go to teacher's college, she is disowned by her father and forced to make her own way. She succeeds in spite of a hasty and disastrous marriage, not only because
she is intelligent, competent, and has a world of practical experience, but also because she is a large (though handsome) and brash

woman, not above thwarting convention and bending rules. Indeed, when she runs away to school she "borrows" clothes and a hat from an older sister that she feels she has earned from her long years of servitude. Kate is not a conventional heroine, and there is much about her physical person and imposing presence that evokes images of the unconventional author herself.

"I think," Kate says in the novel, "that there's not a task ever performed on a farm that I haven't had my share in. I have plowed, hoed, seeded, driven reapers and bound wheat, pitched hay and hauled manure, chopped wood and sheared sheep, and boiled sap; if you can mention anything else, go ahead, I bet a dollar I've done it."[57] In a February 1925 article in *American Magazine* Stratton-Porter mentioned quite a number of other work experiences herself, which prove an extensive education in farming unusual in the average girl's experience, and especially one of her era. But the tone of the article is much different from that of the novel. The article, called "What My Father Meant to Me," virtually canonizes her father. If he may not have been quite the man Stratton-Porter proclaimed him to be, he certainly did provide her with abundant skills for survival and self-sufficiency, and she seemed to have enjoyed and appreciated the process. Shumaker wrote that "as a child Geneva's family duty was to care for the chickens," but he notes that she was free to "wander in the woods, gathering Indian relics, butterflies, moths, and bird feathers, and observing wild life."[58] In *Laddie*, Little Sister's doctor cautions her father to go easy on her. "She isn't cut out for a seamstress or a housewife, Paul. Tell Ruth not to try to force those things on her. Turn her loose out of doors; give her good books, and leave her alone. You won't be disappointed in the woman who evolves."[59] This seems to have been the course that Stratton-Porter's parents took with her and would suggest that the author herself was pretty satisfied with the results.

That is not to say that the author's life lacked personal hardship or plain hard work. In her 1919 *American Magazine* article she disputes the notion that nature study is romantic, insisting that she was accustomed to "work in the fierce sun of July until my arms and shoulders blistered through my clothing. I have waded

Gene Stratton-Porter in her natural habitat and preferred attire.

Jessamyn West, whose novel The Friendly
Persuasion *was a hugely popular book
and was made into a film.*

shallow rivers, crossed on frail rafts at flood time, fought the quicksands of lake shores, worked for days in the slime of swamps and marshes, in high trees, on telegraph poles, amid the unspeakable odors of slaughter-houses and vulture locations, and where I was in danger from vicious cattle and dogs, venemous snakes, and from tramps."[60] The public that devoured her bucolic images of country life never visualized its favorite author covered with mosquito bites, drenched in sweat, standing ankle deep in mud as she pursued the passions that eventually appeared on the printed page in a sanitized version. Despite all the discomforts, inconveniences, and hardships involved in farming, she said of her parents that they simply "loved land, they believed in land, and they lived upon it from choice."[61] The same was true of the author all her life.[62] In *The Harvester* she defends this choice and raises the issue of the ennobling powers of nature when Dr. Harmon, the city dweller, grudgingly admits the superiority of his rival, David Langston, the harvester. "He chose his location. So did I. He is a stronger physical man than I ever was or ever will be. The struggle that bound him to the woods and to research, that made him the master of forces that give back life, when a man like Carey says it is the end, proves him a master. The tumult in his soul must have been like a cyclone in his forest, when he turned his back on the world and stuck to the woods. . . . Some day you must hear. It's a story a woman ought to know in order to arrive at proper values."[63]

It is Stratton-Porter's own life experiences that lend some measure of credibility and veracity to her arcadian tales, just as LeRoy MacLeod's personal knowledge of Indiana farm life makes his novels authentic farm fiction. While other Indiana authors have not written with benefit of such direct experience, several have made noteworthy contributions to agrarian fiction.

In her beloved collection of stories *The Friendly Persuasion*, Jessamyn West tells the story of a Quaker family in southern Indiana during and after the Civil War. The stories are a re-creation of family stories told to her by her mother during Jessamyn's long convalescence. A later West novel about an 1899 Indiana farm, *The Witch Diggers*, is a much darker portrayal.

There is nothing charming about this portrait of an Indiana still in "the Dark Ages."[64]

Maurice Thompson, who merits mention in Meyer's analysis of farm fiction, was another of Indiana's naturalists and outdoor enthusiasts. An engineer and lawyer, Thompson also served for a time as state geologist and head of the department of natural history. He published extensively about outdoor life, sports, and birds. Although he is best known and loved for his romantic novel *Alice of Old Vincennes*, a classic of Indiana literature that enjoyed tremendous national popularity, it was an earlier collection of short stories, *Hoosier Mosaics*, that really launched Thompson's literary career and for which he is given some measure of respect as a local colorist. Most of the stories in the collection are about thwarted romance; however, several are about farmers or country fellows who fall in love with a girl from a class above them, usually a girl from the town or city. Herein lies their chief interest to students of farm fiction. In "The Pedagogue," for example, a feud in print between the schoolmaster and the editor of the local paper divides the community. "Of course it was town against country—the villagers for the editor, the country folk for the pedagogue."[65]

Thompson's farm characters also exhibit the conservatism and independence that Meyer cited as a quality of the rural "type." In his story "Hoiden," a rather reclusive farmer is confronted with the coming of the railroad. "On this particular morning he seemed a little agitated; and, indeed, he was vexed more deeply than he had ever before been. Just the preceding evening he had learned that a corps of civil engineers were rapidly approaching his premises with a line of survey, and that the purpose was to locate and build a railway right through the middle of his farm. To Luke the very idea was outrageous. He felt that he could never stand such an imposition. His land was his own, and when he wanted it dug up and leveled down and a track laid across it he would do it himself. . . . The truth is he was bitterly opposed to railroads, any how. They were innovations. They were enemies to liberty. They brought fashion and spendthrift ways, and speculation, and all that along with them."[66] In the story it is his unrequited crush on the vixenish daughter of the chief engineer that causes him to compromise all his convictions and eventually end up an even lonelier, although wealthier man.

Thompson's deep appreciation for the land does not figure as prominently in his fiction as it does in his nature writing. Some critics, in fact, expressed surprise that *Alice* contained so little description of the physical landscape. Stratton-Porter on the other hand never failed to write her love of land into her novels. "I am a creature so saturate with earth, water, and air," she wrote in the February 1910 issue of *World's Work*, "that if I do not periodically work some of it out of my system in ink, my nearest and dearest cannot live with me."[67]

CHAPTER SIX

Return to Myth

Ross Lockridge, Jr., and the Great American Novel

In his prologue to *The American Adam: Innocence, Tragedy, and Tradition in the Nineteenth Century*, R. W. B. Lewis contends that "the notion of original sin draws its compelling strength from the prior notion of original innocence."[1] While the theme of the lost garden figures everywhere in literature, it is particularly prevalent in American literature because the myth of the new Eden was a fundamental aspect of the American psyche. America represented what the pioneers hoped was nothing less than a new covenant between God and His creation.

Early travel narratives often depicted the New World as an extant paradise, poised for habitation by a new chosen people. As the "garden" proved to be anything but a paradise in the daily experience of settlers, the idea quickly yielded to the dream of creating a garden out of raw wilderness, a paradise of man's own devising, but with God's unquestioned blessing. After the disillusionment wrought upon the American dream by the effects of industrialization, urbanization, and two world wars, the return to a former innocence, or the rediscovery of the myth of the American Eden, became the predominate literary theme in America. It appeared in various guises, all becoming traditional American literary motifs: nostalgia for the past and for the innocence of youth (both of the individual and of the nation), homesickness, and homecoming. All represent an aspect of return to the covenant. All feature heroes, some near-messiah figures, who seek to restore the covenantal relationship.

Perhaps nowhere in American literature is the image of the restorer of the covenant more pronounced than in Ross Lockridge, Jr.'s, *Raintree County*. "My father read America as an experiment that was betraying its early promise,"[2] wrote Larry Lockridge in his Pulitzer prizewinning biography, *Shade of the Raintree*. *Raintree County* was published in 1948, but in the biographer's opinion it was necessary that his father set the novel in the nineteenth century, "when there was still great promise and when humanity had not yet come into the desolation of reality."[3] In his novel Lockridge tried to capture and define exactly what summed up the American myth. And he determined that, essentially, it was "the story of the hero who regains Paradise."[4]

Raintree County on its simplest narrative level is the story of John Shawnessy. It is the Fourth of July 1892 in the small town of Waycross in Raintree County, Indiana, in and around which the middle-aged Shawnessy has spent his entire life. It is the story of one ordinary man's experiences set against the most formative years in American history. Through a series of flashbacks the reader follows Shawnessy from innocent boyhood, through a lost love, a tragic first marriage, his years as a Civil War soldier, and into a comfortable second marriage and middle age. Shawnessy's story is the story of all of humankind: innocence to fall to redemption.

The return of three friends from Shawnessy's youth for the holiday festivities triggers the flashbacks. Jerusalem Webster Stiles, former newspaperman, intellectual, and cynic; Cassius P. Carney, financier; and Sen. Garwood B. Jones represent "types" that illuminate aspects of the American experience and against which Shawnessy seeks to sort out the fundamental meaning of his own life.

The author calls his hero "life's eternal young American,"[5] presumably because, for Lockridge, there was something about the American dream, irrespective of its place of origin, that fulfilled or perfected, at least in potential, the collective dream of all of mankind. Shawnessy, in his search for the meaning of his existence, ultimately finds it in "his mythic participation in the history of the human race from Genesis to Revelation,"[6] as the novelist's biographer put it. "The thing to do," Larry Lockridge wrote, "is to discover the mythical character inherent in any given age or nation or people."[7] In this, he seemed to explain not only what his father was trying to do in *Raintree County*, but also perhaps how he went about it.

Ross Lockridge, Jr., was born in Bloomington, Indiana, in 1914 and died there in March 1948 at the age of thirty-three. He earned a doctorate at Harvard and taught for a time at Simmons College in Boston. Lockridge married his childhood sweetheart and, like his hero, never really desired to distance himself from his hometown.

Lockridge was a complex man, a curious combination of self-doubt and introversion, aggressiveness, and limitless confidence in his novel. He developed a reputation for being difficult in his dealings with publishers and the press, although such disagreeableness was not characteristic according to his family and friends. Likely, Lockridge was so consumed by his novel, the work of seven grueling years, that he never quite got his perspective back and expected everyone with whom he dealt to be equally consumed. He was an optimist and a believer in the American dream, but he was a victim of depression and took his own life by asphyxiation in his car in a closed garage. Lockridge's suicide caused the popularity of his novel to assume epic proportions. The press had a field day trying to sort out the mystery of why a new author whose book had skyrocketed to the top of the best-seller list and had made its poor, young author so much money, as a Book-of-the-Month Club Main Selection and winner of the MGM Novel Award, should take his own life.

Raintree County is, in part, a novel of homecoming, even though Lockridge's hero has more than "a sensation of long absence and return." He has a feeling that "he had [been] reawakened into some earlier time."[8] Shawnessy is more than a hero in this respect; he is both new man and messianic figure, one whose "name had been set upon him like a badge . . . fated to rewrite the great book of God in a new land and in a new tongue."[9]

"America," Shawnessy says in the novel, "is still waiting to be discovered. America is a perpetual adventure in discovery. I've spent my fifty years of life trying to discover America."[10] Lockridge might have used the word *re*discover, for what the author and his character sought to claim was the lost idea of America, the fundamental myths that had inspired generations of pioneers. They wanted to find it, not in the next frontier, but in their own backyards. Lockridge sought to be the epic poet of his place and time.

Lockridge also sought to set his mythic landscape and hero within the whole panorama of mythic history. One of his vehicles was the raintree. His biographer noted the universality of tree worship in primitive cultures and its function in the Genesis story. "Shawnessy's raintree," he wrote, "is a mutation of an ancient archetype, combining trees of life and knowledge in the sacred grove."[11]

Interest in the raintree, of course, preceded Lockridge. It is particularly associated with the New Harmony community, where Thomas Say was supposed to have planted the first tree on the continent. Robert Dale Owen mentions the "shady kolreuteria" in his novel about New Harmony, *Beyond the Breakers*, albeit a bit more matter-of-factly than does Lockridge. "One of the handsomest and most meritorious of ornamental shade trees, growing to the height of thirty or forty feet, introduced into England from China a century ago, and less in use among us than it deserves. In summer its long blossoms cover it like a yellow cloud. Then succeeds a profusion of large seed-vessels—at first red, then yellow, and lastly of a rich brown. It blooms at three or four years old. The villagers, because they had a habit of planting it at their front gates, usually called it the *gate tree*."[12]

Lockridge, too, recited the conventional history of "one of these who brought to New Harmony the seeds of an exotic tree, which he planted by the gate of his house. This tree, bearing the scientific name of Koelreuteria paniculata, had been called the Golden Raintree in its native China. . . . It bore no fruit in the popular meaning of the word, but in late June or early July the mature trees, which seldom grew taller than twenty or thirty feet, bloomed with a delicate yellow flower and dropped a rain of yellow pollendust and petals."[13]

That Lockridge should specify that the tree bore no fruit in the *popular meaning of the word* is the phrase that augurs his departure from the historical record. In spite of, or perhaps in addition to, what he understood to be the purely material history of the tree, Lockridge exploited its mythic value. "According to a popular legend, the earliest settlers found a ragged preacher wandering in the neighborhood of a lake in the middle of the County. He told them that in his youth he had had a vision of Heaven in which he beheld a green land full of fruit-bearing trees and pleasant waters and had gone seeking for its earthly counterpart through the wilderness of America, carrying with him the seed of an oriental tree never before planted in America."[14] In this way Lockridge made his own county the very cradle of the myth.

Henry County, Indiana, the home of the author's mother, was the prototype of the novel's setting though the biographer acknowledges the physical dissimilarities between Raintree County and the "unarresting farmland" of Henry County. "My father enhanced Henry County," he explained, particularly in "lifting" the Eel River from Miami County.[15] More important, Lockridge enhanced it ontologically. He was not as concerned with the corporeal landscape as he was with the landscape of origin and of being. In fact, Larry Lockridge indicates that both the tree itself and the name of the mythic county was a happy coincidence that evolved from the name Henry County. "Saying the word 'Henry' again and again, he stumbled onto 'raintree' by the slight phonetic resemblance. Eureka! The word touched off 'a whole chain of slumbering associations.' " The biographer goes on to say that "since he'd been working with the Edenic myth, 'the motif of the Raintree instantly fused with the already existing pattern of the book. Almost as if by magic the whole landscape of Raintree County . . . sprang into being.' "[16]

Though the raintree is the central metaphor in the novel, a secondary metaphor is the river. "For the river had been there before any man had come," Lockridge writes. "The river was there when the great icesheet withdrew and left the land virginal, dripping, devoid of life. The river was there when the first green life surged up from the south. The river was full of shining fleshes when the first man came wandering into the forest country that was now called Raintree County. And with him man brought names, and the river became a name."[17]

For Shawnessy the river of life, by name, was the Shawmucky, and Lockridge's river prose is often reminiscent in tone of the Genesis story. "Part of the secret was that all things that came from the Shawmucky River were one thing, and all were subtle reminders of himself, and all were perfect in their way, and all had been forever in the river, and the river was the ancient valley of his being, and everything that came from its waters was intolerably beautiful."[18]

The river of life flowed from the formlessness and void of "the great swamp,"[19] and for Shawnessy the river flowed *to* Lake Paradise in Raintree County in Indiana. The uniqueness of Raintree County is that it is Shawnessy's *place* and that the hero seeks the American myth in microcosm there. "That summer, J. W. Shawnessy discovered the Source of Life . . . where the river joins the lake."[20] This is a sense of place at its most fundamental.

What is the way by which souls are plucked from the amorphous swamp and propelled on their individual journeys down the river of life into "the sunlight of Raintree County"?[21] By that most ordinary of human instincts: procreation. Shawnessy's alter ego, "the Perfessor," views the process very pragmatically. "Behold the diagram of Life! . . . At the base of the diagram, there's an immense swamplike womb, and from this rises a giant tree, the umbilicus, through which saplike pours for aeons the stuff of life. Then dangling from this tree in its maturity would be a tiny seedpod, your post-natal individual, whose separation from the parent tree is, biologically speaking, a brief period. Actually we so-called mature individuals are only the pods of the tree, quaintly contrived to seduce one another so that the precious impulse that we carry, the immortal seed, may again and again be shaken back into the swamp of life."[22]

By referring so clinically, almost irreverently, to "your post-natal individual," the Perfessor grossly depersonalizes and demystifies the process. But Shawnessy cannot accept this assessment, and it is through Shawnessy's evolving appreciation for the natural process that it is made mythic.

For Shawnessy, sheer *being* is a miracle. "It is somehow wonderful . . . how life goes on blindly creating itself in the midst of
convulsions."[23] In this stark sexual image he sought to suggest the
broader, more complex "convulsions" of a human life and the persistence of the life force in spite of chaos and human tragedy, eliciting a myth of resurrection as well as homecoming, in the
biographer's view. It is, in fact, what makes Shawnessy a messianic figure, though the biographer admits some reluctance to
extend the theme of resurrection that far.

The central conflict of the story was that the very act by which
life sustains itself was fraught with guilt and remorse and laden
with consequences. Shawnessy, of two natures, "had always par-
ticipated in two worlds. One was the guiltless earth of the river of
desire, the earth big with seed, the earth of fruit and flower. The
other was the world of memory and sadness, guilt and duty, loyalty and ideas."[24] The fruit of the tree of knowledge.

The young Shawnessy succumbs to a drunken sexual encounter
with a woman he does not love and barely knows. Through her
duplicity, his sense of honor, and the pressure his mother and
social conventions bring to bear on him, Shawnessy marries, with
tragic consequences for all involved. Societal constraints prove to
be an ironic catalyst in this regard. America, Lockridge wrote,
"was always an education in self-denial. And Raintree County was
itself the barrier of form imposed upon a stuff of longing, life-jet of
the river."[25]

The barrier of form is a recurrent theme in Lockridge's novel.
The masculine impulse to chart the course of rivers (and presumably the course of one's own life), to impose linear, geometrical
forms upon the land, is set against the randomness and mystery
of nature that Lockridge views as feminine. "Man made an atlas
for the earth . . . with straight lines—ranks of corn, telegraph
poles, rectangular walls—he tried to overcome its feminine evasions."[26] It is through feminine evasions that the early course of
Shawnessy's life is determined and from which he struggles to
extricate himself.

Women represent the greatest mystery to Shawnessy.
Throughout the novel, passive adjectives and elusive, enigmatic

Infamous dust jacket from Raintree County *with the not-so-hidden "recumbent female form."*

feminine images are contrasted with crude, bluntly masculine action words, as when Shawnessy as a soldier contemplates Lookout Mountain and Missionary Ridge. He perceives them as "great breasts of earth, colossally feminine and passive. For the possession of this couched shape, immense, brooding, silent, he and his comrades must fight, retch, shriek, bleed, die."[27]

A secondary metaphorical quest throughout the novel is the search for an old atlas of the county that was believed to contain hidden lewd images within its illustrations of common landmarks. This sophomoric pursuit anticipated the excitement inspired by the novel itself, whose dust jacket contained the form of a naked reclining woman, shaped by the hills, valley, and the contours of "the fullbodied river."[28] As with most optical illusions, once the woman becomes apparent, she is quite obvious, and she never again cannot be seen. For the problem, as Shawnessy saw it, was that "the formal map of Raintree County had been laid down like a mask on something formless, warm, recumbent, convolved with rivers, undulous with flowering hills, blurred with motion, green with life. He mused upon this mingling of man's linear dream with the curved earth, couched in mystery like a sphinx."[29]

The feminine curve of the earth and of the river, whose "strange meeting . . . with the illusory [male] rectangle of Raintree County"[30] made it a mythical place, was why "people will hunt it on the map, and it won't be there."[31] For Lockridge, the map of America should be a "map that is like a face or a human form."[32] It is history, the history of "all the faces of mankind that had passed briefly through the world of time and space. Flowerlike they rose—like flowers springing and like dense flowers falling and fading back into the swamp."[33] The only meaningful form is "the mystic shape of a life upon the land,"[34] of an individual in his or her place.

It is the day when Shawnessy plunges naked into the Shawmucky that he finally feels free from "the geometry of fences, roads, and railroads . . . re-entering some ancestral part of himself."[35] It is at the moment of his sexual encounter with Susanna on the banks of the river that "it . . . seemed to him dimly that he had thrust his way to the secret heart of life."[36] And, as after finding the image in the atlas, he could never again see anything but that warm, recumbent formlessness, or seek anything but the mystery of his own origins. For he knew that "it was all here, the same plentiful and peaceful earth. All the old symbols were here, the tokens of the legend, waiting to be read. The great enigma was here, murmuring its lost language among the rushes at the river's edge."[37]

In *Raintree County* the reader encounters the same imperious images of nature that have permeated so many other Indiana novels. While for Shawnessy they are ultimately life-affirming, for the jaded, cynical figure of the Perfessor it is all "muck."[38] For the secret, as far as the Perfessor was concerned, was that "ugly and beautiful, like moral and immoral, are unknown to the Republic of the Great Swamp, which really doesn't give a hang who your forebears were. It only cares that the seed be sifted back into the muck so that the little faces will pop out again, year after year, generation after generation, and seduce each other like flowers, innocently and promiscuously."[39]

That innocence and promiscuity should be conjoined in Lockridge's schema was what caused such furor at the release of the novel. Everywhere throughout Raintree County, both the novel and the fictional place, is profound sensory evidence of the predominance of the natural order. "The lifegiving waters are odorous with the flesh of fish and trees rotten with rains."[40] Elsewhere in the novel "the creatures of the river swarmed, shrieked, swam, coupled, seeded, bloomed, died, stank around him. He appeared to be in the very source of life, a womblike center."[41] The odors of Lockridge's garden are the natural odors of the sex act, birth, and decay. The sexual imagery in Raintree County—penetration, fecundity, wetness, virginity, subjugation, and conquest—is also the imagery of wilderness and of life.

The predominance of nature has another aspect in nature's tendency to reclaim its own. Leonard Lutwack, in *The Role of Place in Literature*, calls it "the idea of vegetative re-conquest." According to Lutwack, "the decay of civilization may be effectively symbolized by the recrudescence of vegetation in civilized places, especially within houses and cities."[42] Lockridge's unsettling image of a country graveyard as "a formal garden of death, which life was slowly reclaiming to formless fecundity,"[43] is a striking representation of this theme. Throughout *Raintree County* the hero grapples with the circular processes of life and death, but nowhere more profoundly than in the graveyard scene. "In the middle of orderly cornlands, it was an island of disorder. He kicked up crowds of grasshoppers as he walked through uncut grass, gravemyrtle, wild carrot, white top, blackberries, poison ivy . . . life rushed up from the breasts of the dead in a dense tangle of stems that sprayed seeds and spat bugs . . . doomed and huddled shapes around which green waters were steadily rising. He stood up to his knees in grass and weeds, holding in one hand a box of peaceful cut flowers and in the other a sickle."[44]

The flowers represent a tribute to the power and victory of death, a peace offering or even the white flag of surrender. The sickle is the symbol of man's unwillingness to surrender to the ultimate victory of nature. Lutwack noted that "excessive vegetation," represents to "the civilized man, . . . too abundant life and too insistent sexuality,"[45] and that "stripping landscape of vegetation is like the ravishment of the female."[46]

Be that as it may, "too insistent sexuality" was why many readers and critics faulted the novel. Of numerous writers who have used sexuality to interpret the Genesis myth, perhaps none has been more intentional and direct than was Lockridge. When Shawnessy and Susanna "sin" beside Lake Paradise they have eaten of "forbidden fruit." They "put on clothes and with them shame and a sense of guilt,"[47] and they swim back across the lake "feeling as if an eye were watching them from covert."[48] Shawnessy fails to notice that they lay beneath a tree that rained "a dust of yellow flowers . . . on his shoulders and into the black hair of the girl."[49] He knows only that he left behind his hero's oak-leaf garland, won in a race that day, and with it, his innocence.

It is significant that this pivotal incident occurred on the shores of Lake Paradise because Lockridge contends that "here . . . the father and mother of mankind walked alone and naked . . . [and ate] long ago . . . of the delectable flesh of the fruit of the golden tree."[50]

Though ultimately Shawnessy regains a measure of paradise in the quiet domesticity of his second marriage, his regard for his

second wife, Esther, can never match the youthful exuberance
and innocence of his passion for the unattainable Nell, for whom
the unfortunate Susanna had been a poor, momentary substitute.
"The young man . . . had been lost there beneath the Raintree and
had never come back."[51] Still, by gaining a comfortable compan-
ionship into which he can settle with his musings and reminis-
cences, "he had overcome the aloneness of the garden."[52] Of the
much younger Esther, Lockridge writes: "On an unsuspected path
he had found her waiting. He had helped to fashion her, and yet
she had lain at the very sources of himself. In her, he had redis-
covered Eve."[53]

Lest the reader should miss the idea that in Esther, who interestingly enough has Native American blood, Shawnessy rediscov-
ers Eve, "her name was being called in the garden . . . in the cool
of the evening."[54] Even the snake makes an appearance, Esther
having stepped on "a long lewd fellow, writhing under her very
feet" as she encounters Shawnessy on that unsuspected path in
the early stages of their acquaintance. "She had touched this
green and yellow monster with her naked foot, and here she was
now helpless in his domain, in the very sink and center of it."[55]
Green and yellow are the signature colors of the landscape of
Raintree County and representative of its fertility ("the green
blood of life").[56] Esther has set foot, quite literally, upon the path
of her own loss of youth and innocence.

For the garden is simultaneously the center of God's creation
and the serpent's habitat. At the end of the novel the hidden picture is spotted in the atlas. On the illustration of the front of the
county courthouse "the stern yet necessary lady with the scales,
whose upright form had ruled the conscience of Raintree County"
had been replaced with "the father and mother of mankind in
beautiful nakedness, tasting the Forbidden Fruit!"[57]

The play of light through trees always evokes a mystical quality
in literature and is no less evocative in *Raintree County*. "Looking
upward he saw the sunburst of the tree in the very middle of the
sacred grove,"[58] writes Lockridge of his "Adam." This is the very
grove where "in making love to Susanna under the raintree and
paying for it mightily, he [Shawnessy] lives out the Genesis

myth,"[59] according to Lockridge's biographer. Larry Lockridge contends that *Raintree County* was a novel in which his father tried "to express the American myth, building on the Garden of Eden and the Fall of Man."[60] Ross Lockridge attempts more than building upon "the oldest story in the world."[61] He attempts fulfillment of it in a narrative that parallels the childhood, ministry, and passion of Jesus, with allusions to the entry into Jerusalem and his arrest. "When the child had grown in years and strength,"[62] Shawnessy writes of himself in his own legend of Raintree County, the short legend that appears at the end of the novel and neatly encapsulates Shawnessy's quest, "which was no other than to win eternal life from darkness and a dream of darkness."[63] The novel is full of scenes where Shawnessy "withdrew from the crowd"[64] or where he "anticipated this coming of torches through the night."[65] The reader can visualize palm branches waving with the exclamations "Make way, make way for the Hero of Raintree County!"[66] As a soldier, Shawnessy knows that "these old hills would have their solemn immortality, fashioned from his bloody anonymity."[67] And finally, reminiscent of the tomb, "in the dark earth lay the rejected seed."[68]

Raintree County is an orgy of scriptural imagery, but it is the earthly aspect of the Jesus figure that Lockridge explores most fervently. Fertility images are more presupposing than even the ripe biblical metaphors in *Raintree County*. For Lockridge the garden was the natural condition, the intended state of humanity, and procreation the natural response of man. There was "something about the climate of Raintree County,"[69] after all, "the pollenous air." It was "an auroral and maternal earth."[70] Golden fruit, forbidden fruit was "temptingly displayed in the garden of Raintree County."[71] By the end of the novel Shawnessy's comfortable middle age has tempered the sexual vitality of his youth. But Shawnessy retains the memory of a time when "love was a flower that wanted to tear its tassel and scatter its ecstasy of seed in spring beside the river."[72] A time when "there was . . . only Johnny Shawnessy . . . his hair stiff with seed."[73] It is the journey back to childhood memories of joy and of innocence.

Lockridge's hero realizes in the course of his journey that the value of myths can be lost in the finding, as surely as the condition of innocence is lost in knowledge. "I don't know that it would do any good to find it," Shawnessy laments regarding the raintree. "It's funny, but I've made a myth out of that tree, and I don't want to destroy the myth. Somehow, that tree embodies the secret of life, the riddle of Raintree County, and yet I know it's not the physical tree itself that embodies it, and I don't want to disillusion myself."[74]

The search for a mythical place that does not exist on any map, and the disillusionment inherent in the reality, was the theme of another novel, roughly contemporaneous with *Raintree County*. "There was nowhere such as I dreamed," Marguerite Young writes in *Miss MacIntosh, My Darling*.[75] "That which I had come so far to find . . . the Wabash country, seemed far away, the landscape of a dream which should not be dreamed in the Wabash country, for it should not be realized but in another place."[76]

Young was born in Indianapolis in 1908, attended Manual Training High School, and earned her bachelor's degree from Butler University. She taught English at Shortridge High School during the 1930s and taught for a time at Indiana University after receiving her master's degree from the University of Chicago. Young lived in New York for most of her adult life, and she died in Indianapolis in 1995.

Young first met success as a poet. She earned some critical attention for her prose in 1946 with the publication of *Angel in the Forest*, a lyrical, mythical interpretation of the New Harmony experiment. But it was not until *Miss MacIntosh, My Darling* that Young gained an abiding place in American literature.

Miss MacIntosh is the story of Vera Cartwheel, who sets out by bus to find her childhood nurse, Miss MacIntosh of What Cheer, Iowa, who had been her only stable influence growing up at the mercy of an opium addict mother, who was probably also schizophrenic. The delusions, hallucinations, and parade of imaginary houseguests that inhabit Catherine Cartwheel's haunted existence have rendered the narrator unable to distinguish between reality and illusion, and she clings to a memory of Miss MacIntosh and a vision of the Midwest that is dashed as she passes through Indiana at night in a torrential downpour. The coiling complexities of the plot and characters and the multiple symbolisms defy brief description and confound the basic narrative. Nothing is as it seems in this novel or in the narrator's experience. Miss MacIntosh proves to be bald and missing a breast, both of which realities she has carefully concealed from Vera and the world under the illusion of wig and prosthesis.

While Lockridge employs two major mythic symbols, the tree of knowledge and the river of life, Young experiments with literally hundreds, the most substantive of which are fruit and water. The name MacIntosh is ripe with mythic associations.

> Less than the contributions of her old MacIntosh forefathers who had given the apple and the rainproof both, the macintosh that grew on the rosey boughs of the old Iowa and all through the temperate zone from sea to shining sea and was good for cooking or eating raw, just as the frugal housewife saw it, and was not the same apple that caused our corruption, the macintosh being no fruit in Eden on the Tree of Knowledge and not mentioned either in the annals of Babylon or in the Egyptian Book of the Dead, the macintosh being not those golden apples falling upward, the macintosh being found nearest the tree from which it fell, a very simple product for physical sustenance only and bone-building and keeping fit and entirely adequate to its purposes outside of purgatory like, indeed, that other macintosh, also bequeathed by canny Scots, this very rainproof she wore and which covered sailors in the deep and in the storm and was more practical throughout all this known world than this very same old Emperor Constantine or any other emperor shedding his tears like pearls upon the curtain of fog she walked through, black umbrella lifted, buffeting under the wheelings of sea-birds crying like foghorns, the firmament of water laid upon water.[77]

It is instructive that Miss MacIntosh's forebears are credited with an article of protection from the elements, just as Miss

MacIntosh was herself the narrator's refuge throughout the storm of her childhood. To the narrator Miss MacIntosh was "as the Rock of Ages in a land where all things crumbled, as a guide who knew her way, as the acme of common sense, as the sure-footed Pilgrim . . . as the one person who was simple and bold and clear."[78] For Miss MacIntosh, from that "temperate zone" of the Midwest, was herself, like the apple, a "simple product for physical sustenance . . . and entirely adequate to its purposes."

For Lockridge water was a predominantly creative element, the source of life, "that transparent restorer of our strength, which God has lavished upon mankind in such copious quantities."[79] In *Miss MacIntosh*, water is a destructive principle, the ultimate weathering agent of human habitation and hope. In the land-locked region of the Midwest, far from the threat of hurricane, high tides, and the perils of the open seas, to which the young narrator is at least accustomed, rain and floods wreak their own distinctive havoc. The narrator is startled by the drenched and dismal scene barely visible through the bus window as she surveys the depleted Indiana landscape. The Midwest that she has desperately anticipated as a refuge—"that land of promise through eternity, there where the trees would blossom and where no flower would fade, there where the children would dance, where the young would not grow old, where the old would never die"[80]—is nowhere visible.

Instead, the devastation wrought by the rain amplifies the devastation already wrought by human disregard, compounding the sense of displacement, insubstantiality, and chaos that the narrator has sought to ameliorate by her journey. "These vacant lots piled up with rusted chassis and broken wheels and flat tires, bedsprings like old musical instruments never to be played on again, sodden mattresses, old pillows which had lost their feathers, old football helmets, loving cups which would gather nothing but the rain."[81]

Throughout the novel images of emptiness, negligence, and decay abound in the rural Indiana landscape where "the streets were splotched as if with rain or a disease. There were signboards lurching and indistinct and vacancy as if there were not even a

facade between ourselves and nothingness hanging on nothingness, and there were patches of the almost iridescent winter
weeds which had lasted into the spring of the year and grew
between the broken pavements, and there were pools of standing
water."[82]

For the narrator, coming from the eastern seaboard where water
is active, unpredictable, and often unmanageable, where it does
everything but stand, standing water is representative of the most
contemptible aspects of complacent midwestern existence. On
the other hand, Miss MacIntosh had been a fish out of water during her sojourn on the East Coast where she was "so unaccus-
tomed to this invidious sea damp which crept into old manor
houses within the sound of the invading sea, the dampness of the
air tarnishing the silver and making the gold peel in curls off the
picture frames, the near proximity of the loathsome surf which,
with her flattest Middle Western manner about her, she com-
plained of."[83] Miss MacIntosh's superior midwestern disapproval of
all things eastern and pretentious gives her a special satisfaction
at the decline of the great New England house by the sea. In her
humble opinion, "that this rich man's castle should slip gradually
into ruins . . . was perhaps the best of penalties which could be
devised by careless nature."[84]

Throughout the novel, as indeed throughout all of Young's
poetry and prose, the question of what is dream and what is reality, of illusion and of organic life, is played out again and again.
Therefore the rain-drenched landscape seemed like both "the
beginning of creation,"[85] and "the end of the world."[86]

In *Raintree County* the dream is trapped within the reality, cry-
ing for release. In *Miss MacIntosh* the dream is both reality and
illusion, at the same time, as if existing in parallel universes. Both
novels are stories of journey and of return. The similarities
between the two novels, diverse as they are in subject matter, go
well beyond the material realities that both were considered by
many critics to approach the Great American Novel, that other elusive myth, and that both were the subjects of elaborate spreads in
Life magazine.[87] Both novels were daunting in their sheer volume
of words and depth and breadth of subject, while being limited in

their basic narrative structures to very short time frames—one day in the case of *Raintree County*, and what has been called "the longest bus ride in history"[88] in the case of *Miss MacIntosh*. *Miss MacIntosh* was an astonishing 1,198 pages and took over seventeen years to write. *Raintree County* was a respectable 1,060 pages and consumed seven years of its author's life. Both authors were adept at stream-of-consciousness "lists" or litanies of images that attempted to capture the essence, as well as to display the panorama of human myth and history in near encyclopedic proportions. Both novels exhibited a style that was intensely psychological, operating on many levels of consciousness and perception. Neither was chronological, and each was faulted for being repetitious and excessive, while at the same time being praised for "cumulative force" and "cumulative . . . power."[89] Both novels have been characterized as deeply metaphorical and metaphysical, intensely biblical in their imagery and lyricism. Both authors have been compared repeatedly to James Joyce. Both novels could be described as "nothing for the average, casual reader to pick up on a warm day."[90]

The average reader approaches both novels with the same trepidation with which he or she might face *Ulysses*. In an article in *Vogue* in 1946, which appears in *Inviting the Muses*, a collection of essays and short stories published in 1994, Young recalls her own encounter with the novel. "When I first read Joyce's *Ulysses*, I felt as if I were under an ether mask—but after all, there was a pattern, a curious logic."[91] The same can be said of *Miss MacIntosh*. Though there are many patterns, a logic can be gleaned and appreciated from even the briefest encounter with it. It can be read almost piecemeal as prose poetry; it can be skimmed for a superficial appreciation of its solid grounding in the Midwest.

In *Inviting the Muses*, Young discusses a work in progress, "a three-volume epic on the life and times of Eugene Victor Debs, of which the canvas is the millennial or I should say the failed millennial continent of America with its most unusual fate which was to be that of the lost earthly paradise to be restored by socialism in terms of man's quest for the perfect or almost perfect world—

the Jasons' golden bough or tree of golden apples in the Garden of Eden sometimes glimpsed but not yet discovered or restored."[92]

Like Lockridge, Young was concerned that "our age is devoid of one informing myth."[93] While she herself called her style "rococo,"[94] and her prose was and is criticized for its exhaustive ornateness, it was necessary to the tumultuous interplay of illusion and human reality. "We need the myth of infinite distended variety," she wrote in *Inviting the Muses*, "to combat the spiritual vacuity which our unthinking technicians have presented to us and which they will continue to present. A static concept of world and idea would be repellent to those who understand the great change wrought in our universe by the release of the atomic bomb."[95]

The same need was expressed by Joseph L. Blotner in his review of *Raintree County* in the winter 1955–56 issue of *The Western Humanities Review*. "This novel is . . . remarkable when it is seen in the perspective of its own time. When other novelists were writing of the desolation of war, of the disillusionment of its aftermath, and of the destruction of old values and orders, Ross Lockridge made an all-consuming effort whose total effect was a reaffirmation of faith in America and the American dream."[96]

Another Indiana novelist, Marthedith Furnas, explored the myth of the garden, but also, perhaps unwittingly, the perils of being consumed by mythmaking. "The perception of this kind of beauty," she writes in *A Serpent's Tooth*, "is the perception of anything standing still so that you can see it exactly as it is, and with the perceiver standing still so that he can become a pure recording instrument. It is possible therefore only in the brief condition of security, walled around by the care of some Lord God or other in the days of His strength. Those fixed and final forms, that motionless perceiver, have never existed. But to everybody they seem to have, since everybody has been a child."[97]

Hoosier novelist Kurt Vonnegut, Jr., also explored the theme of the garden and the innocent perceptions of childhood. In *God Bless You, Mr. Rosewater*, Indiana again becomes an Eden when, at the very end of the novel, Eliot decides to make every child in Rosewater, Indiana, his heir. " 'Let their names be Rosewater from this moment on. And tell them that their father loves them . . . and tell them,' he began again, 'to be fruitful and multiply.' "[98]

There is little ground between innocence and insanity. Vonnegut's endearing eccentric finally gains "the garden," but it appears in yet another guise. "Everything went black for Eliot, as black as what lay beyond the ultimate rim of the universe. And then he awoke to find himself sitting on the flat rim of a dry fountain. He was dappled by sunlight filtering down through a sycamore tree. . . . Eliot was within a high garden wall, and the garden was familiar . . . it was the garden of Dr. Brown's private mental hospital in Indianapolis."[99]

Lockridge did his own stint in a mental ward. Ironically, Lockridge had sought to reintroduce myth and the *redeeming* qualities of mythmaking because to him, as his son writes, art "should be offering a therapy." Instead, so far it had failed "to communicate our collective myths and history."[100] Perhaps Lockridge felt that he, too, had failed in this regard. Perhaps his greatest vulnerability was his intense emotional engagement in the miracle of being. If he could have achieved and maintained the state of "pure recording instrument," perhaps his prodigious talent could have redeemed him.

CHAPTER SEVEN

That Particular Ground

Contemporary Literature and the Sense of Place

In Meredith Nicholson's *A Hoosier Chronicle* a character speaks wistfully of his boyhood in the Adirondacks, and through him, Nicholson conveys his own deeply felt sense of place and of how it impacts human character, as well as of the power of the written word to convey it. "When I strike Adirondacks in print I put down my book and think a while. It's a picture word. It brings back my earliest childhood as far as I can remember. I call words that make pictures that way moose words; they jump up in your memory like a scared moose in a thicket and crash into the woods like a cavalry charge."[1]

The reader could make a parlor game of the many words that might have been for Nicholson and others "moose words," familiar images used by generations of Indiana writers to stimulate memories and to convey a sense of atmosphere, a sense of place.

Sense of place has been given so much attention in recent years as to suggest that the idea is something new in regional writing. Far from being a creation of contemporary writers, place has been a critical component of the spoken and written word since human history began.

It can be said of the early local-color movement that a realization of regional uniqueness and a sense of the value of place to the human story contributed enormously to the evolution of American literature, a literature otherwise as vast, diverse, and unwieldy as the continent itself. The romancers who chose to experiment with Indiana as a setting for their tales of romance and adventure, and the early realists such as Tarkington who

sought to capture a unique and vanishing physical and social landscape for posterity, contributed to a growing regional literature as
well. The agrarians who were advocates for a renewed appreciation for the physical landscape in an age that glorified the urban
landscape, and the mythmakers, such as Lockridge, who explored
the ideas of time and space that help shape the reality, added
another dimension to the literary landscape of Indiana. A generation of writers in exile addressed the condition of exodus and of
return, and many contemporary writers, for whom Indiana represents rich and limitless opportunities to explore the whole of the
human condition in microcosm, might prove to represent a whole
new level of literary regionalism.

In *The Role of Place in Literature*, Leonard Lutwack contends
that man's perception of himself is always in relation to his surroundings and that "the most elemental orientation of a reader to
a narrative text is through its evocation of places."[2]

Just as important as the place setting of a narrative is the place
identity of the author, which always, even if by omission or avoid-
ance, informs a narrative. "A writer must have a place . . . to love
and be irritated with," Louise Erdrich writes in *A Place of Sense:
Essays in Search of the Midwest*. "Location, whether it is to abandon it or draw it sharply, is where we start."[3]

Theodore Dreiser was driving through Warsaw, Indiana, when
he was profoundly struck by this realization. "Right here," he
wrote in *A Hoosier Holiday*, "I began to ponder on the mystery of
association and contact, the chemistry and physics of transfer-
ence by which a sky or a scene becomes a delicious presence in
the human brain or the human blood, carried around for years in
that mystic condition described as 'a memory' and later transferred, perhaps, or not, by conversation, paint, music, or the written word, to the brains of others, there to be carried around again
and possibly extended in ever widening and yet fading circles in
accordance with that curious, so-called law . . . of the transmuta-
tion of energy."[4]

Another Indiana author, Kurt Vonnegut, Jr., for all his sometimes curmudgeonly references to the Indiana of his youth,
stresses as a central theme of his work the importance of com-

munity, of extended family, and of "home." "The members of . . .
a society," Vonnegut wrote in *Fates Worse than Death*, "must feel
that a particular piece of land gave birth to them, and has been
and always will be theirs."[5] For Vonnegut, it is precisely the eclips-
ing of this most primitive and fundamental human need that
accounts for the malaise of modern society. In *Fates* he directly
addresses the reader. "Isn't your deepest understanding of time
and space and, for that matter, destiny shaped like mine by your
earliest experiences with geography, by the rules you learned
about how to get home again?"[6]

While Vonnegut addresses this issue repeatedly in essays, inter-
views, and autobiographical "collages," he approaches it more
obliquely in his novels, only one of which, *God Bless You, Mr.
Rosewater*, is set in Indiana, but most of which include characters
from Indiana and references to the state. For Vonnegut Indiana
seems to be a pretty convenient place for a character to have been
from, either to convey a quality of innocence and wholesomeness,
or an absolute rusticity and lack of sophistication.

" 'My God,' a stranger addresses the protagonist in *Cat's Cradle*,
'are you a Hoosier?'

I admitted I was.

'I'm a Hoosier, too,' she crowed. 'Nobody has to be ashamed of
being a Hoosier.'

'I'm not,' I said. 'I never knew anybody who was.'

'Hoosiers do all right. Lowe and I've been around the world
twice, and everywhere we went we found Hoosiers in charge of
everything.'

'That's reassuring.' "[7]

Vonnegut's character, far from considering herself a "stranger,"
insists that Hoosiers must stick together. "Whenever I meet a
young Hoosier, I tell them, 'You call me *Mom*.' " This groping for
connection, however tenuous and contrived, Vonnegut views as a
"textbook example of a false karass, of a seeming team that was
meaningless in terms of the ways God gets things done,"[8] every bit
as arbitrary as the government-issued middle names in *Slapstick*
that randomly link a person with tens of thousands of imposed
"relatives" of the same middle name. Such devices represent the

desire to be something more than "interchangeable parts in the American machine,"[9] the basic human need to belong, gone haywire, as everything goes in Vonnegut.

Vonnegut belongs to a generation of American writers who explore and deplore the homogenization of American culture, the loss of identity and of mission not only of a particular town, city, or region, but of an entire nation and, indeed, species. In *Breakfast of Champions* he picks on Holiday Inn as a symbol of the new American "neutrality," of a "brotherhood" of "thousands upon thousands of rooms in Holiday Inns all over the world. . . . Dwayne Hoover might be confused as to what his life was all about, or what he should do with it next. But this much he had done correctly: He had delivered himself to an irreproachable container for a human being. It awaited anybody."[10]

In this way Vonnegut adds a dimension to a time-honored literary theme. There need be no ambivalence, no angst, no pathos in the idea of returning home. "The past has been rendered harmless," a character in *Breakfast of Champions* quips. "I would tell any wandering American now, 'Of course you can go home again, as often as you please. It's just a motel.' "[11]

A legacy of provincialism, lethargy, and limitations has become associated with life in the Midwest. In Dan Wakefield's *Going All the Way* two Korean War veterans returning home to Indianapolis in the fifties find themselves unprepared for the sterility, small-mindedness, and insularity of their hometown. In one revealing episode friends discuss the possibility of moving to California.

" 'We live *here*,' said Peachie, 'in Indianapolis.'

'There isn't any law says you have to,' Gunner said.

'There isn't any law says we have to leave, either.'

'But why do you have to stay?' Gunner asked.

'It's home,' she said. 'It's where we live.' "[12]

The same narrow, unimaginative attachment to place appears in the fiction and nonfiction of Indiana writer Susan Neville. In an essay in *Indiana Winter* she describes an older couple's trip to Europe. "They went to Germany a couple of years ago. . . . The brakes went out on his rental car while he was in Europe, and he drove from Italy to Germany pulling on the emergency brake whenever he needed to stop.

"When I got back, he said, I told the guys I wouldn't trade Indiana for ten Germanies. . . . You know we weren't made, Merle said, to fight against our natures."[13]

In Dreiser's short story "The Lost Phoebe" a farmer and his wife are utterly contained, physically and spiritually, by the boundaries of their Indiana farm. "The orchard, the meadow, the cornfield, the pig-pen, and the chicken-lot measure the range of their human activities. . . . All the rest of life is a far-off, clamorous phantasmagoria, flickering like Northern lights in the night, and sounding as faintly as cow-bells tinkling in the distance."[14]

Lutwack defends the literary and human value of a fixed or focused experience of place. "Intensification of plot and theme," he writes in *The Role of Place in Literature*, "are aided when all action and imagery are concentrated in a central place . . . [a] kind of centripetal force in literature."[15] Regional literature has always made use of the power of this force to focus the vast human drama most sharply on the smallest of stages.

Images of "home," perhaps the most universal of "moose words," are as varied as they are compelling, but the aspect they all seem to share is that of a memory of innocence and a realization of the loss of innocence and the desire to return to it.

In *The Passionate Shepherd*, a wonderful collection of short stories set in Indiana and published in 1957, former Indiana University English professor Samuel Yellen explored the different manifestations of home, identity, and of return. In one of the most compelling stories, "Vergilian Vespers," the adult Vergil Shelley returns to Mantua, Indiana, because his mother is dying of cancer. Although he refers to himself as "Ishmael," he nevertheless confesses his exile to be "self-imposed."[16] In one of the most poignant scenes in the story Vergil uncovers an old schoolbook in which he had once "written with blue ink in the awkward hand, the hackneyed boyish seeking after identity:

Vergil Shelley
Grade 10
Home Room 21

Mantua High School
Mantua
Mantua County
State of Indiana
United States of America
Continent of North America
Western Hemisphere
The Earth
Solar System
Milky Way
The Universe"[17]

In the title story of Yellen's collection, a stuffy college professor decides to disappear, to simply abandon wife and family, and to live anonymously in a rooming house on the west side of what is obviously Bloomington. He takes a manual labor job in a stone quarry, and a whole new worldview is opened to him. In one episode he recounts "the thrill I felt one morning when, clinging shakily to the iron cables, I took my first ride on a huge block of limestone swung high in the air by the derrick. All around me the sheer limestone walls dazzled my eyes with a brilliant display of color. I had not known that there could be so many tints of brown and yellow and orange and purple in such a variety of strippling and shading."[18]

In another Yellen story set near Bloomington, "Stoneville Pike," the central character, returns home to find things "queerly different . . . from the way he remembered it . . . things seemed displaced, landmarks were not where they should have been."[19] He sits for hours on a once-familiar bluff contemplating a small dam. "Now in the midsummer hardly any water dribbled over it, and the pool looked stagnant. But *then*, in that *ago*, in that fabulous spring time, a Niagara had poured over and the pool had rippled with fresh water. Well, there it was, a thing stale and sluggish like himself."[20]

In one fashion or another all of Yellen's characters seek that "ago," the place or places that in memory, and only in memory, are "an oasis in the desert of time. An island in the swift-flowing stream."[21] In "Vergilian Vespers" Vergil walks a street from his childhood, "one of the few left in Mantua with the original side-walks of red bricks laid in marquetry pattern, no longer straight and level, but twisting, pitching, and buckling, like the carapace of a Jurassic lizard, over the roots of the old trees."[22] Like childhood memories buckling over the roots of change.

In a much earlier collection of stories called *An Idyl of the Wabash and Other Stories* published in 1899, Indiana author Anna Nicholas explored the ideas of place and placelessness in a story called "An Itinerant Pair," which is set in Michigan City, Indiana. In this story an itinerant Methodist minister and his wife are viewed with a mixture of pity and suspicion by local townsfolk for their lack of a home. The minister acknowledges the sacrifice that his calling has made necessary. "We could not set our hearts upon this house or that tree, as people will. The room where the son died or the daughter married could not be kept sacred, for we must leave them; the roses and the vines which we might plant would grow to gladden other eyes than ours."[23] And yet, in this story the couple is happy. They possess inner resources that the villagers do not. The latter may have houses, but they are built upon the proverbial (and quite literal) sand. While the itinerants have the freedom to move on, the townsfolk are prisoners of place, represented by the looming image of the actual prison. "In every direction was sand—mountains of sand, valleys of sand. It was in drifts upon the sidewalks, in hillocks in the streets. The houses were built upon it. . . . The scattering tufts of grass in the front yards seemed to have given over the ambition to cover the earth with green, and were creeping under the sand. Did I imagine a burden in the air, as of grief or guilt? The shadow of the prison seemed to hover over the place. It grew oppressive."[24]

Nicholas uses the dryness and insidiousness of sand to reflect the unsubstantiality of human habitation. Dust figures in Susan Neville's story "The Invention of Flight," in the collection of the same name, in which the narrator lives "in a town slowly turning into dust. Choked, finally, by the fields which surround it and by a larger town a few miles west which kept growing like a fat old man adding chocolate to chocolate who, one night in bed, rolled

In delivering the tenth-annual Marian McFadden Memorial Lecture in 1986, Vonnegut told a North Central High School crowd that they would become mature beings, and happier ones, if "you realize that your lives are not supposed to be stories, only stories are supposed to be stories."

over and gently, quietly crushed his wife. The dust is from the houses rotting, the streets unpaved and rotting, pollen thick as fog, grain elevators pouring out the slick sweet dust of rotting corn until that time in the fall when the fields become white and brittle as bleached bones and the corn is cut close to the roots."[25]

The destructive element is water in Michael Martone's essay in *A Place of Sense* in which a community endures the seasonal cycle of floods that reconfigures its landscape. "Fort Wayne floods are slow disasters," Martone writes, "with people going to work as usual while others pump their basements or fill sandbags. There is always plenty of warning. There is always nothing to be done."[26]

Nearly equal to the force of nature is the force of human carelessness. Perhaps nowhere is this idea so forcefully put forth as in William Gass's 1968 collection *In the Heart of the Heart of the Country*. Gass indicts the Midwest in general, but the town of "B" in Indiana particularly, for a neglect recognizable to any Hoosier who views the rural Indiana landscape with anything like objectivity. "Many small Midwestern towns are nothing more than rural slums" populated by folks who "undertake makeshift repairs with materials that other people have thrown away; paint halfway round their house, then quit; almost certainly maintain an ugly loud cantankerous dog and underfeed a pair of cats to keep the rodents down. . . . They will collect piles of possibly useful junk in the back yard, park their cars in the front, live largely leaning over engines, give not a hoot for the land, the old community, the hallowed ways."[27]

Whether it is Gass's "rural slums" or the "shithouses, shacks, alcoholism, ignorance, idiocy and perversion"[28] of Vonnegut's *God Bless You, Mr. Rosewater*, the Midwest of many contemporary writers is bleak, flat, and colorless. In the recent collection of essays, *Writing from the Center*, Bloomington, Indiana, author Scott Russell Sanders states that "if I had to draw up a short list of regional qualities, I would include flatness, fertility, austerity, conformity, civility—and their opposites. None is unique to the Midwest, of course, since the qualities of any region will be variations on those common to America at large. But the combination is distinctive, arising from geography as much as from history."[29]

Yet for Sanders and other contemporary Indiana writers there
is a unique "richness in long-settled, cultivated, often battered
and abandoned country [which] is the special calling of
Midwestern writers."[30] Flatness has figured prominently in Indiana
literature from its earliest writers. In Neville's short story "Johnny
Appleseed," a drifter enters a woman's life and offers all kinds of
magical possibilities, but she is initially immune to his seduction.
"The earth is flat here, I said. It looks flat, he said, but it's really
bending; it has to, you know, it has to bend everywhere. Not
around here, I said. A circle bends everywhere, he said; it appears
flat like the earth, but it's really bending. It's flat, I said. Very, very
flat."[31]

Martone suggests that flatness "informs the writing of the
Midwest."[32] For some authors flatness suggests dullness. For
others it suggests, perhaps, sameness and predictability, which to
the midwestern temperament is not the same thing and is
not necessarily a liability. Lutwack defends this midwestern
conservatism in *The Role of Place in Literature*. "Lacking
the unknown potential of heights and depths, flat places are safe,
restful, reassuring."[33]

In *Raintree County* Corporal Shawnessy hates the Tennessee
landscape. "He was a man from the flat country, and he now perceived a new beauty in the level of Raintree County. It tranquil-
lized the spirit, it was the image of space, it suggested civilization
and good roads. It meant peace and plenty and contentment."[34]

The midwestern preference for continuity and predictability
has become a staple element of humor about the region and also
a popular aspect of Hoosier character for novelists and short story
writers. It is only one, and by far the most benign, of many images
that have come to be associated with Hoosier character. The
Indiana of literature too often has been populated by slack-jawed,
shoeless cretins who spit tobacco juice and refer to their state as
"Injanny," by toothless women and old "yaller" dogs, by corn
pone, bacon, and sassafras tea. Often the Indiana of literature has
been characterized by a myopic political and religious conservatism, racial prejudice, and xenophobia. The Hoosier of literature is often suspicious of anyone who eats with a fork instead of

a knife and drinks from a cup instead of the "sasser." The Hoosier of literature is more than a little put off by anyone who reads anything other than the Bible and an almanac, with the possible exception of *Pilgrim's Progress*.

Contemporary authors such as Elizabeth Arthur have present-day equivalents of such Hoosier idiosyncrasies. In *Binding Spell*, a wonderfully wacky novel about a witch, a small-town sheriff, lots of dogs, and kidnapped Russian professors, Arthur captures small-town isolationism. "The town of Felicity, like other contrary towns in Indiana, had decided years before to scorn the idea of Daylight Savings Time—unimaginative muffins, these people could not seem to take pleasure in the simplest flights of fancy, and insisted that if it was time at all, it had always to be the same."[35] The unflattering images of Indiana in this novel are the observations of an outsider, an eighty-one-year-old Hungarian widow who has inherited an Indiana farm and who finds the small community mystifyingly inhospitable.

High Cotton by Darryl Pinckney also gives the perspective of an outsider, a young black man in the Indianapolis of the sixties who moves to the suburbs and ultimately escapes to New York. The narrator remembers, among other Indianapolis cultural phenomena, the 500-Mile Race. " 'White Trash Day,' Grandfather called it . . . a tradition of beer cans thrown from passing cars, white Pat Boone shoes, checkered trousers, white belts, increased highway fatalities, and condoms peeking up in the reservoirs like water moccasins."[36]

Pinckney's characters make the move from Capitol Avenue to the suburbs, pursuing their fair share of the American dream. But upward mobility like theirs is viewed as an offensive campaign by the white Indianapolis of the fifties in Dan Wakefield's *Going All the Way*. "Every time Sonny came home from college or the Army he heard the latest report on how far *They* had advanced out of their old small, crowded, rickety bastion. The ominous *They*, like some relentless army, crept north past one parallel block after another, destroying real-estate values as they went, as brutally as Sherman laid waste the property of Georgia in his march to the sea."[37]

Sometimes negative literary images of Indiana are impressions of non-Hoosiers who have come to live in the state, or who pass through it on their way to or from other places. Sometimes such images are the memories of embittered and superior exiles, or the honest reflections of native sons returned with a new and broader perspective. In each case it is an outside perspective.

The viewpoint of the returned prodigal is perhaps the most instructive and ultimately satisfying because it would seem to be the most insightful. Lutwack calls it "critical views of the familiar place."[38] The "critical" view, in the sense of penetrating or discerning, is not necessarily critical in the sense of disparaging. Nicholson and Tarkington were authors who made good use of the wandering hero who returns educated, experienced, and worldly-wise, with a new appreciation for the old hometown and its now-proven values. This motif, Lutwack suggests, "creates a feeling of stability and completion."[39] The hero has seen the world and has made a conscious choice to return to his or her place of origination. Readers are expected to benefit by the experience of the hero, without having to risk the journey themselves.

The themes of escape and of return are integral to American literature. Lutwack contends that "one might posit a whole conception of American literature turning on the conflict of the desire to remain fixed in a paradisal place and the impulse toward motion."[40] One might even extend this conception by suggesting that midwestern literature in particular is one of exodus, exile, and return. In large part this is because midwestern provincialism and predictability is so pronounced that the literary hero, and vicariously the reader, *must* escape, even if only temporarily. Sometimes there is a "sense of superiority as an escaped Midwesterner."[41] But return is also a device by which defenders of the region and its values justify their defense. In *Writing from the Center* Scott Russell Sanders states that "many characters who identify with the Heartland see the country most clearly from the windows of trains or buses or cars, from the decks of rafts or boats, from horseback or wagon bed or motorcycle, for to a striking degree the literature of the Midwest has been one of arrivals and departures."[42] Ronald Weber saw this midwestern theme as "a central ambivalence" that "has enriched its literature."[43]

Real place value happens when images of a region or lifestyle resonate on a sensory level with readers. Michael Martone is masterful at a casual depiction of familiar landscapes, characters, and scenarios that joggle the reader's memory without assaulting it. When Martone describes the regulars in the local diner who stack their own dishes after eating, the Hoosier reader recognizes them. When he recalls the seasonal preoccupation with tornadoes, the reader recalls it too. "I remembered feeling this way every spring and summer—too hot, too still. You can hear better. There was this picture in the grocery store . . . of a drinking straw driven into the trunk of an elm."[44]

In her short story "The Fairfield Poet," Mary Hartwell Catherwood long ago demonstrated the power of a few small sensory images to evoke memories. "Fireflies were filling one field, as if a conflagration under that particular ground sent up endless streams of sparks. She smelled the budding elders, and was reminded of tile-like bits in her past, fitted oddly together."[45]

The attention to small details of a Neville or Martone is vastly different from the contrived recitation of place-names that lesser writers often mistake for regional flavor. A handful of detective and romance novels are set in Indianapolis. Sometimes the city barely masquerades under imaginary, and unimaginative, names such as Capitol City or Circle City. Sometimes the city appears as itself . . . ad nauseam. Michael Z. Lewin's *Ask the Right Question* is a good example of a droning litany of minutiae of time and place that is, to some extent, characteristic of the detective novel as a genre. At one point in the novel, for example, Lewin's protagonist decides to do some research at the public library. "I gathered my notebook and writing instrument and went out for a leisurely stroll. West down Ohio Street to Pennsylvania Avenue. Then north up Pennsylvania. The route took me through Indianapolis's ideological heartland. Within oblique sight of the Soldiers and Sailors Monument in the Circle. . . . Past the post office and Federal Building, the *Star-News* Building and the YWCA. . . . And finally to St. Clair Street. Where I entered, at long last, the Indianapolis-Marion County Public Library. . . . I headed immediately for the microfilm files of the Arts Division on the second floor. There are six microfilm viewers on the south wall of the Arts Division. But at that time in the morning there wasn't much demand for them, so I got one of the two at the right, next to the microfilm cabinets."[46]

One can scarcely imagine what interest any of this information might be to the reader from outside central Indiana, as it bears no real relationship to the plot. Perhaps the author wanted to gratify his hometown audience. Perhaps the style was a deliberate imitation of the terse, clipped sentence fragments which are the stock-in-trade of crime writers. This would account for such devices as the use of the term "broad" for woman, "in the a.m." for morning, and "writing instrument" for pen or pencil.

Crime writer Ronald Tierney indulges in the same kind of geographical name dropping in his Deets Shanahan series. Deets is an Indianapolis detective with a healthy appetite. In *The Iron Glove* Tierney mentions "Sakura's, the Japanese restaurant on Keystone Avenue," and "Cafe Patachou on Forty-ninth and Pennsylvania."[47] In *The Stone Veil*, it is René's in Broad Ripple (having "the best potato salad in the world"),[48] and in *The Steel Web* he mentions Fletcher's, Jonathan's Keepe, Chateau Normandy, and Peter's.[49] In *The Steel Web* Tierney also mentions the strip bars on Pendleton Pike, though not, interestingly, by name. In *The Iron Glove* Tierney even refers to Donna Mullinix's society column in the local paper, a reference so current that it may well mean nothing to even local readers in a few short years. Such trendiness is certainly not a quality of enduring regional literature, which Weber characterized as "work that distinctly arises from place yet remains uncontained by place."[50] Genre novels such as those of Tierney and Lewin are distinctly contained by place, what Weber would have called "*mere* regionalism" as opposed to real regionalism.[51]

What can be said about even such literature, however, is that it does recognize and attempt to satisfy a genuine hunger for regional flavor. The so-called modern novel was so profoundly influenced by naturalism as to have been, in some cases, rendered utterly placeless. In the first few pages of *Miss MacIntosh,*

Marguerite Young put it so: "There was now no landscape but the soul's, and that is the inexactitude, the ever shifting and the distant."[52]

In addition to the dictates of a literary vogue, other aspects of modern society—mobility, mass media, anonymity, uniformity, alienation, breakdown of the nuclear family—have contributed to a rather sterile and despairing literary perspective with regard to man and his meaning. In *Fates Worse than Death*, Vonnegut referred to "the Great American experiment" as "an experiment not only with liberty but with rootlessness, mobility, and impossibly tough-minded loneliness."[53] One weapon in the struggle to restore individual self-identities would seem to be restoring a sense of shared regional identity and pride of place.

As the frontier of the romancers pushed west and ultimately met the sea, it yielded to the "urban wilderness" of naturalism and finally to the landscape of the mind in the modern novel. Interior spaces opened up vast new dimensions of time and place to writers such as Vonnegut who explore the frontiers of fantasy and of psychosis. And yet, somehow, most have proven to be somewhat dissatisfying to the contemporary reader.

If contemporary writers can imbue a particular place, however humble, with some sense of uniqueness, of individuality, of specialness, then they can conceivably help readers make sense of their own place in a diffuse society. In *Writing from the Center* Sanders notes that "for the writer, for anyone, where you live is less important than how devotedly and perceptively you inhabit that place."[54]

It is in this respect, finally, that all Indiana writers, past and present, of whatever genre, movement, or form, stand or fall. To the extent that any of them, from Eggleston to Tarkington to Lockridge, truly inhabited his or her place, truly perceived it with all its foibles and grotesqueries, but also with all its transcendence and mythic power, to that extent they have blessed Indiana readers with a distinct literary identity and contributed to the rich and diverse landscape of American literature.

Notes

Preface

1. Christian J. Bay, ed., *Native Folk Spirit in Literature* (Cedar Rapids, Iowa: Friends of the Torch Press, 1957), 10.

Introduction

1. James Hurt, *Writing Illinois: The Prairie, Lincoln, and Chicago* (Urbana: University of Illinois Press, 1992), 1.
2. William Coyle, ed., *Ohio Authors and Their Books, 1796–1950* (Cleveland and New York: The World Publishing Company, 1962), xv–xvi.
3. Ibid., xvii.
4. Hurt, *Writing Illinois*, 3.
5. Wilson O. Clough, *The Necessary Earth: Nature and Solitude in American Literature* (Austin: University of Texas Press, 1964), 82.
6. Leonard Lutwack, *The Role of Place in Literature* (Syracuse, N.Y.: Syracuse University Press, 1984), 31.

1. Moral Geography

1. Marion T. Jackson, ed., *The Natural Heritage of Indiana* (Bloomington: Indiana University Press, 1997), xvii.
2. Marthedith Furnas, *The Night Is Coming: A Novel* (New York: Harper and Brothers, Publishers, 1939), 9.
3. George Barr McCutcheon, *Viola Gwyn* (New York: Dodd, Mead and Company, 1922), 18.
4. Jessamyn West, *Leafy Rivers* (New York: Harcourt, Brace and World, 1967), 94.
5. Ibid., 11.
6. Gene Stratton-Porter, *Freckles* (New York: Grosset and Dunlap, 1904), 8–9.
7. Janet Flanner, *The Cubical City* (New York: G. P. Putnam, 1926), 18.
8. Ibid., 52.
9. Charles Major, *A Forest Hearth: A Romance of Indiana in the Thirties* (New York: The Macmillan Company, 1903), 17.
10. Kate Milner Rabb, ed., *A Tour through Indiana in 1840: The Diary of John Parsons of Petersburg, Virginia* (New York: Robert M. McBride and Company, 1920), 78–79.
11. George C. Eggleston, *Jack Shelby: A Story of the Indiana Backwoods* (Boston: Lothrop, Lee and Shepard Company, 1906), 56.
12. Jessamyn West, *The Massacre at Fall Creek* (New York: Harcourt Brace Jovanovitch, 1975), 349, 350.

13. James M. Hiatt, *The Test of Loyalty* (Indianapolis: Merrill and Smith, 1864), 165.

14. George Barr McCutcheon, *Kindling and Ashes; or, the Heart of Barbara Wayne* (New York: Dodd, Mead and Company, 1926), 6.

15. Marthedith Furnas, *A Serpent's Tooth* (New York: Harper and Brothers, 1946), 77.

16. Gene Stratton-Porter, *A Girl of the Limberlost* (New York: Doubleday, Page and Company, 1909), 318.

17. Kathleen Wallace King, *The True Life Story of Isobel Roundtree: A Novel* (Little Rock, Ark.: August House Publishers, 1993), 77.

18. Michael P. Kube-McDowell, *Alternities* (New York: Ace Books, 1988), 233.

19. Frank A. Myers, *Thad Perkins: A Story of Early Indiana* (London: F. Tennyson Neely, 1899), 120.

20. James Baldwin, *In My Youth: From the Posthumous Papers of Robert Dudley* (Indianapolis: The Bobbs-Merrill Company, 1914), 5.

21. George C. Eggleston, *Jack Shelby*, 88.

22. Baynard Rush Hall, *The New Purchase; or, Seven and a Half Years in the Far West*, James A. Woodburn, ed. (Princeton, N.J.: Princeton University Press, 1916), 191. Originally published by D. Appleton, 1843. A second edition appeared in 1855, which omitted about 130 pages related to President Andrew Wylie. The Princeton edition, the most useful, contains an introduction by James A. Woodburn.

23. Ibid., 192.

24. LeRoy Armstrong, *The Outlaws: A Story of the Building of the West* (New York: D. Appleton and Company, 1902), 19.

25. Ibid., 20.

26. Hall, *New Purchase*, 208.

27. Myers, *Thad Perkins*, 120.

28. Simon Schama, *Landscape and Memory* (New York: Alfred A. Knopf, 1995), 227.

29. Leonard Lutwack, *The Role of Place in Literature* (Syracuse, N.Y.: Syracuse University Press, 1984), 166.

30. Baldwin, *In My Youth*, 8.

31. Jessamyn West, *The Friendly Persuasion* (New York: Harcourt, Brace and World, 1940), 97.

32. Ibid., 101.

33. Nancy N. Baxter, *The Movers: A Saga of the Scotch-Irish* (Austin, Tex.: Guild Press, 1987), 87.

34. Edward Eggleston, *The Circuit Rider: A Tale of the Heroic Age* (London: George Routledge and Sons, 1874), 102.

35. Edward Eggleston, *The Graysons: A Story of Illinois* (New York: The Century Company, 1887), 116.

36. Ibid., 113.

37. Hall, *New Purchase*, 367.

38. Caroline Brown, *Dionis of the White Veil* (Boston: L. C. Page and Company, 1911), 199.

39. Ibid., 201.

40. Ibid., 74.

41. West, *Friendly Persuasion*, 99.

42. Lutwack, *Role of Place in Literature*, 32.

2. Pride and Protest

1. Arthur W. Shumaker, *A History of Indiana Literature, Indiana Historical Collections*, vol. 42 (Indianapolis: Indiana Historical Bureau, 1962), 154, 156.

2. Ibid., 155.

3. Baynard Rush Hall, *The New Purchase; or, Seven and a Half Years in the Far West*, James A. Woodburn, ed. (Princeton, N.J.: Princeton University Press, 1916), 182.

4. Ibid., 389.

5. Ibid., 51.

6. Ibid., 458.

7. Ibid., 3.

8. Ibid., 49.

9. Ibid., 485.

10. Ibid., 87.

11. Ibid., 61.

12. Ibid., 70–71.

13. Ibid., 70.

14. Ibid., 124.

15. Ibid., 61.

16. Ibid., 81.

17. Ibid., 372.

18. Ibid., 335.

19. Ibid., 347.

20. Ibid., 348.

21. Ibid., 350–51.

22. Ibid., 190.

23. Leonard Lutwack, *The Role of Place in Literature* (Syracuse, N.Y.: Syracuse University Press, 1984), 56.

24. Hall, *New Purchase*, 1.

25. Ibid., 191.

26. Frank A. Myers, *Thad Perkins: A Story of Early Indiana* (London: F. Tennyson Neely, 1899), 163.

27. Hall, *New Purchase*, 191.

28. John A. Jakle, *Images of the Ohio Valley: A Historical Geography of Travel, 1740 to 1860* (New York: Oxford University Press, 1977), 54.

29. Ibid.

30. Hall, *New Purchase*, 209 n.1.

31. Shumaker, *History of Indiana Literature*, 154.

32. Eunice Beecher, *From Dawn to Daylight; or, the Simple Story of a Western Home* (New York: Derby and Jackson, 1859), 49.

33. Ibid., 161.

34. Ibid., 245.

35. Ibid., 60.

36. Ibid., iii.

37. Shumaker, *History of Indiana Literature*, 168.

38. *Indianapolis Times*, 9 December 1936.

39. *Indianapolis News*, 10 November 1906.

40. Beecher, *From Dawn to Daylight*, 151.

41. Ibid., 50.

42. Ibid., 53.

43. Ibid., 140.

44. Fred Lewis Pattee, *A History of American Literature since 1870* (New York: The Century Company, 1915), 258.

45. Ibid., 258.

46. R. E. Banta, comp., *Indiana Authors and Their Books, 1816–1916* (Crawfordsville, Ind.: Wabash College, 1949), 54.

47. Shumaker, *History of Indiana Literature*, 301.

48. Ibid., 302.

49. Ibid., 303.

50. Mary Hartwell Catherwood, *The Queen of the Swamp, and Other Plain Americans* (Boston: Houghton Mifflin, 1899), author's note.

51. Ibid.

52. Banta, comp., *Indiana Authors and Their Books, 1816–1916*, p. 55.

53. Mary Hartwell Catherwood, "Lilith," *Lippincott's Magazine* (January 1881): 35.

54. Ibid., 30.

55. Catherwood, *Queen of the Swamp*, 184.

56. Ibid., 155.

57. Mary Hartwell Catherwood, "Mallston's Youngest," *Lippincott's Magazine* (August 1880): 189.

58. Catherwood, *Queen of the Swamp*, 155.

59. Catherwood, "Mallston's Youngest," 194.

60. Shumaker, *History of Indiana Literature*, 304.

61. Ibid., 305.

62. Ibid., 304.

63. Pattee, *History of American Literature since 1870*, p. 262.

64. Ima Honaker Herron, *The Small Town in American Literature* (New York: Haskell House Publishers, 1939), 201.

65. William Randel, *Edward Eggleston* (New York: Twayne Publishers, 1963), introduction.

66. Ronald Weber, *The Midwestern Ascendancy in American Writing* (Bloomington and Indianapolis: Indiana University Press, 1992), 27.

67. Ibid., 38.

68. Donald Kay, "Infant Realism in Eggleston's The Hoosier Schoolmaster," *The Markham Review* (February 1971): 81.

69. Edward Eggleston, *The Hoosier School-Master* (Bloomington: Indiana University Press, 1984), preface. Originally published in book form by Orange Judd, New York, 1871.

70. Edward Eggleston, "Formative Influences," *The Forum* 10 (November 1890): 286.

71. Ibid., 286.

72. Weber, *Midwestern Ascendancy in American Writing*, 11.

73. Pattee, *History of American Literature since 1870*, p. 98.

74. Effa Morrison Danner, "Edward Eggleston," *Indiana Magazine of History* 33 (December 1937): 453.

75. Eggleston, *Hoosier School-Master*, 81.

76. Edward Eggleston, *Duffels* (New York: D. Appleton and Company, 1893), 91.

77. Edward Eggleston, *Roxy* (New York: Charles Scribner's Sons, 1878), 74.

78. Ibid., 405.

79. Eggleston, *Hoosier School-Master*, 133.

80. Ibid., 11.

81. Ibid., 12.

82. Ibid., 24.

83. Ibid., 39.

84. Ibid., 141.

3. When Knighthood Was in Flower

1. Fred Lewis Pattee, *The New American Literature, 1890–1930* (New York: The Century Company, 1930), 76.

2. Alfred Kazin, *On Native Grounds: An Interpretation of Modern American Prose Literature* (New York: Reynal and Hitchcock, 1942), 10.

3. Ibid., 13.

4. Ibid., 13, 53.

5. Ibid., 13.

6. *Indianapolis Star*, 9 January 1910.

7. Simon Schama, *Landscape and Memory* (New York: Alfred A. Knopf, 1995), 60.

8. Charles Major, *The Bears of Blue River* (1901; reprint, Bloomington: Indiana University Press, 1984), 267. Originally published by Doubleday and McClure, 1901.

9. Ibid., 277.

10. Ibid., 273–74.

11. Ibid., 32–33.

12. Ibid., 206.

13. Ibid., 162.

14. Charles Major, *A Forest Hearth: A Romance of Indiana in the Thirties* (New York: The Macmillan Company, 1903), 14–15.

15. Booth Tarkington, *The Gentleman from Indiana* (New York: Doubleday and McClure Company, 1899), 6.

16. Ibid., 82.

17. Ibid., 1.

18. Ibid., 382.

19. Ibid., 299.

20. Walter L. Fertig, "Maurice Thompson as a Spokesman for the New South," *Indiana Magazine of History* 60 (December 1964): 326.

21. Maurice Thompson, *Alice of Old Vincennes* (Indianapolis: The Bowen-Merrill Company, 1900), introductory note to M. Placide Valcour.

22. Ibid., 4.

23. Maurice Thompson, *Hoosier Mosaics* (New York: Garrett Press, 1969), 7. First published by E. S. Hale and Son, 1875.

24. Richard R. Roberts, "The Literary Life of George Barr McCutcheon," *Indianapolis Star Magazine*, 26 April 1964, p. 45.

25. George Barr McCutcheon, *The Sherrods* (New York: Grosset and Dunlap, 1903), 16.

26. Ibid., 28.

27. Ibid., 35.

28. Ibid., 87.

29. Ibid., 101.

30. Ibid., 156.

31. Ibid., 168.

32. Ibid., 193.

33. Ibid.

34. Ibid., 196.

35. Ibid., 198.

36. Ibid., 216.

37. Review of *The Sherrods, The Reader* (December 1903): 104.

38. George Barr McCutcheon, *Viola Gwyn* (New York: Dodd, Mead and Company, 1922), 45.

39. Ibid., 62.

40. Ibid., 29.

41. *Indianapolis Star*, 11 December 1910. "Very Howellsy" means that an attempt is made to depict the small details of day-to-day life.

42. Ibid.

43. Meredith Nicholson, *The House of a Thousand Candles* (New York: Grosset and Dunlap, 1905), preface.

44. Ibid., ii.

45. Ibid., 61.

46. Ibid., 19.

47. Ibid., 23.

48. Ibid., 44.

49. Ibid., 57.

50. Meredith Nicholson, *A Hoosier Chronicle* (Boston and New York: Houghton Mifflin Company, 1912), 172.

51. Ibid., 6.

52. Ibid.

53. Ibid., 7.

54. Review of "And They Lived Happily Ever After," *Indianapolis News*, 18 September 1925.

55. Unattributed newspaper article, Indiana State Library biography files.

56. Nicholson, *Hoosier Chronicle*, 605.

57. Meredith Nicholson, *Otherwise Phyllis* (Boston and New York: Houghton Mifflin Company, 1913), 5.

58. Ibid., 353.

59. Ibid., 375.

60. Dorothy Ritter Russo and Thelma Lois Sullivan, *Biographical Studies of Seven Authors of Crawfordsville, Indiana* (Indianapolis: Indiana Historical Society, 1952), 110.

61. Keith J. Fennimore, *Booth Tarkington* (New York: Twayne Publishers, 1974), 42.

62. Thompson, *Alice of Old Vincennes*, 59.

63. Ibid., 102.

64. Theodore Dreiser, *An American Tragedy* (Cleveland: The World Publishing Company, 1925), 833.

65. Kazin, *On Native Grounds*, 230.

66. William E. Wilson, *Indiana: A History* (Bloomington and London: Indiana University Press, 1966), 206–7.

4. The Mark of the Machine

1. Meredith Nicholson, *Old Familiar Faces* (Indianapolis: The Bobbs-Merrill Company, 1929), 149.

2. Arthur W. Shumaker, *A History of Indiana Literature, Indiana Historical Collections*, vol. 42 (Indianapolis: Indiana Historical Bureau, 1962), 354.

3. Keith J. Fennimore, *Booth Tarkington* (New York: Twayne Publishers, 1974), chronology.

4. *Indianapolis News*, 29 July 1939.

5. Robert C. Holliday, *Booth Tarkington* (Garden City, N.Y.: Doubleday, Page, 1918), 47.

6. Booth Tarkington, "As I Seem to Me," *Saturday Evening Post*, 2 August 1941, p. 47.

7. James Woodress, *Booth Tarkington: Gentleman from Indiana* (Philadelphia and New York: J. B. Lippincott Company, 1954), 182.

8. Vernon Louis Parrington, *The Beginnings of Critical Realism in America, 1860–1920*, vol. 3 of *Main Currents in American Thought, An Interpretation of American Literature from the Beginnings to 1920* (New York: Harcourt, Brace and Company, 1930), 375.

9. Booth Tarkington, *The Midlander* (Garden City, N.Y.: Doubleday, Page and Company, 1924), 1.

10. Booth Tarkington, *The Turmoil* (New York: Harper and Brothers Publishers, 1915), 6.

11. Ibid., 85.

12. Ibid., 283.

13. Ibid., 1.

14. Ibid., 2.

15. Ibid., 82.

16. Ibid.

17. Ibid., 6.

18. Ibid., 113.

19. Booth Tarkington, *The Magnificent Ambersons* (New York: Grosset and Dunlap Publishers, 1918), 98.

20. Fennimore, *Booth Tarkington*, 98.

21. Tarkington, *The Midlander*, 488–89.

22. Ibid., 493.

23. Booth Tarkington, *Alice Adams* (Garden City, N.Y.: Doubleday, Page and Company, 1921), 28.

24. Ibid., 94.

25. Ibid., 81.

26. Ibid., 423.

27. Ibid., 432.

28. Ibid., 433.

29. Theodore Dreiser, *Dawn* (New York: Horace Liveright, 1931), 156.

30. Blanche Housman Gelfant, *The American City Novel* (Norman: University of Oklahoma Press, 1954), 42.

31. Dreiser, *Dawn*, 65.

32. William E. Wilson, *Indiana: A History* (Bloomington and London: Indiana University Press, 1966), 223.

33. Alfred Kazin, *On Native Grounds: An Interpretation of Modern American Prose Literature* (New York: Reynal and Hitchcock, 1942), 45.

34. Parrington, *Beginnings of Critical Realism in America*, 354.

35. Philip L. Gerber, *Theodore Dreiser Revisited* (New York: Twayne Publishers, 1992), 120.

36. John Lydenberg, "Ishmael in the Jungle," in *Dreiser: A Collection of Critical Essays*, John Lydenberg, ed. (Englewood Cliffs, N.J.: Prentice-Hall, 1971), 30.

37. Ibid., 31.

38. Ronald Weber, *The Midwestern Ascendancy in American Writing* (Bloomington and Indianapolis: Indiana University Press, 1992), 67.

39. Ibid., 55.

40. Lydenberg, "Ishmael in the Jungle," in Lydenberg, ed., *Dreiser*, 27.

41. H. L. Mencken, "The Dreiser Bugaboo," in ibid., 80.

42. Weber, *Midwestern Ascendancy in American Writing*, 52.

43. Shumaker, *History of Indiana Literature*, 18.

44. Theodore Dreiser, *A Hoosier Holiday* (New York: John Lane Company, 1916), 261.

45. Ibid., 16.

46. Ibid., 231.

47. Dreiser, *Dawn*, 107.

48. Theodore Dreiser, *The "Genius"* (New York: Garden City Publishing Company, 1915), 118.

49. Dreiser, *Dawn*, 174.

50. Dreiser, *The "Genius,"* 220.

51. Ibid., 221.

52. Donald Pizer, comp., *Critical Essays on Theodore Dreiser* (Boston: G. K. Hall and Company, 1981), 286.

53. Gelfant, *American City Novel*, 94.

54. David Graham Phillips, *Susan Lenox, Her Fall and Rise* (New York: Appleton and Company, 1917), 239.

55. Kazin, *On Native Grounds*, viii, ix.

5. "So Saturate with Earth"

1. Ruth Suckow, "Middle Western Literature," *English Journal* 21 (March 1932): 176.

2. Henry Nash Smith, "The Western Farmer in Imaginative Literature, 1818–1891," *The Mississippi Valley Historical Review* 36 (December 1949): 481.

3. Wilson O. Clough, *The Necessary Earth: Nature and Solitude in American Literature* (Austin: University of Texas Press, 1964), 17.

4. Smith, "The Western Farmer in Imaginative Literature," 484.

5. Ronald Weber, *The Midwestern Ascendancy in American Writing* (Bloomington and Indianapolis: Indiana University Press, 1992), 3.

6. Roy W. Meyer, *The Middle Western Farm Novel in the Twentieth Century* (Lincoln: University of Nebraska Press, 1965), 146.

7. Ibid., 13.

8. Leonard Lutwack, *The Role of Place in Literature* (Syracuse, N.Y.: Syracuse University Press, 1984), 154.

9. Ibid., 156.

10. Caroline B. Sherman, "The Development of American Rural Fiction," *Agricultural History* 12 (January 1938): 67.

11. "Thomas Boyd Joins the Rush Back to the Farm," *New York Times Book Review*, 30 August 1925, p. 8.

12. "An Iowa Farm," ibid., 5 October 1930, p. 6.

13. Sherman, "The Development of American Rural Fiction," 67.

14. Weare Holbrook, "The Corn Belt Renaissance," *The Forum* 72 (July 1924): 118.

15. Meyer, *Middle Western Farm Novel in the Twentieth Century*, 6.

16. Ibid., 8.

17. Ibid., 153.

18. Ibid., 164.

19. Ibid., 174.

20. Weber, *Midwestern Ascendancy in American Writing*, 14.

21. Edward Eggleston, *The Graysons: A Story of Illinois* (New York: The Century Company, 1887), 39.

22. Meyer, *Middle Western Farm Novel in the Twentieth Century*, 152.

23. Lutwack, *Role of Place in Literature*, 176.

24. LeRoy MacLeod, *The Crowded Hill* (New York: Reynal and Hitchcock, 1934), 33.

25. LeRoy MacLeod, *The Years of Peace* (New York: The Century Company, 1932), 227.

26. *Indianapolis News*, 28 November 1934.

27. Meyer, *Middle Western Farm Novel in the Twentieth Century*, 7.

28. Alfred Kazin, *On Native Grounds: An Interpretation of Modern American Prose Literature* (New York: Reynal and Hitchcock, 1942), 7.

29. MacLeod, *Crowded Hill*, 49.

30. Ibid., 168.

31. MacLeod, *Years of Peace*, 85.

32. Ibid., 10.

33. Ibid., 258.

34. Ibid., 223.

35. Ibid., 224.

36. Ibid., 121.

37. Ray Allen Billington, *Land of Savagery, Land of Promise: The European Image of the American Frontier in the Nineteenth Century* (Norman: University of Oklahoma Press, 1981), 175.

38. MacLeod, *Years of Peace*, 6.

39. Meyer, *Middle Western Farm Novel in the Twentieth Century*, 11.

40. MacLeod, *Crowded Hill*, 158.

41. Ibid., 212.

42. Ibid., 128.

43. Ibid., 290.

44. Ibid., 170.

45. Ibid., 181.

46. Ibid., 189.

47. One must also extend the period of time under discussion by a decade or so in each direction.

48. Judith Reick Long, *Gene Stratton-Porter: Novelist and Naturalist* (Indianapolis: Indiana Historical Society, 1990), 1.

49. Ibid., 2.

50. Gene Stratton-Porter, *A Daughter of the Land* (Garden City, N.Y.: Doubleday, Page and Company, 1918), 7–8.

51. Arthur W. Shumaker, *A History of Indiana Literature, Indiana Historical Collections*, vol. 42 (Indianapolis: Indiana Historical Bureau, 1962), 412–13.

52. Ibid., 412.

53. Gene Stratton-Porter, "Why I Always Wear My Rose-Colored Glasses," *American Magazine* (August 1919): 118.

54. Long, *Gene Stratton-Porter*, 159–60.

55. Ibid., 175.

56. Stratton-Porter, *Daughter of the Land*, 3–4.

57. Ibid., 171.

58. Shumaker, *History of Indiana Literature*, 405.

59. Gene Stratton-Porter, *Laddie: A True Blue Story* (Gardern City, N.Y.: Doubleday, Page and Company, 1913), 109.

60. Stratton-Porter, "Why I Always Wear My Rose-Colored Glasses," 117.

61. Ibid., 37.

62. Even after Stratton-Porter moved to Hollywood to participate in the filming of her novels, she always escaped to the country to recharge and had just built two secluded country homes in California at the time of her death. She continued to explore, preserve, and write about local flora and fauna wherever she lived.

63. Gene Stratton-Porter, *The Harvester* (New York: Grosset and Dunlap, 1911), 389. Originally published by Doubleday, Page and Company, 1911.

64. Jessamyn West, *The Witch Diggers* (New York: Harcourt Brace, 1951), 144.

65. Maurice Thompson, *Hoosier Mosaics* (New York: Garrett Press, 1969), 175.

66. Ibid., 131.

67. Gene Stratton-Porter, "Why I Wrote 'A Girl of the Limberlost,' " *World's Work* (February 1910): 12545.

6. Return to Myth

1. R. W. B. Lewis, *The American Adam: Innocence, Tragedy, and Tradition in the Nineteenth Century* (Chicago: University of Chicago Press, 1955), 9.

2. Larry Lockridge, *Shade of the Raintree: The Life and Death of Ross Lockridge, Jr.* (New York: Viking, 1994), 203.

3. Ibid., 234.

4. Ross Lockridge, Jr., *Raintree County* (New York: Penguin Books, 1994), 886. Originally published by the Houghton Mifflin Company, 1948.

5. Ibid., 188.

6. Larry Lockridge, *Shade of the Raintree*, 276.

7. Ibid., 229.

8. Ross Lockridge, Jr., *Raintree County*, 53.

9. Ibid., 55.

10. Ibid., 294–95.

11. Larry Lockridge, *Shade of the Raintree*, 294.

12. Robert Dale Owen, *Beyond the Breakers: A Story of the Present Day* (Philadelphia: J. B. Lippincott and Company, 1870), 248.

13. Ross Lockridge, Jr., *Raintree County*, 44–45.

14. Ibid., 43–44.

15. Larry Lockridge, *Shade of the Raintree*, 10.

16. Ibid., 243.

17. Ross Lockridge, Jr., *Raintree County*, 95.

18. Ibid., 107.

19. Ibid., passim.

20. Ibid., 257.

21. Ibid., 1021.

22. Ibid., 306.

23. Quoted in Larry Lockridge, *Shade of the Raintree*, 212.

24. Ross Lockridge, Jr., *Raintree County*, 259.

25. Ibid., 116.

26. Ibid., 41.

27. Ibid., 657.

28. Ibid., 204.

29. Ibid., 7.

30. Ibid., 155.

31. Ibid., 848.

32. Ibid., 736.

33. Ibid., 314.

34. Ibid., 8.

35. Ibid., 93.

36. Ibid., 266.

37. Ibid., 1041.

38. Ibid., 315.

39. Ibid.

40. Ibid., 396.

41. Ibid., 103.

42. Leonard Lutwack, *The Role of Place in Literature* (Syracuse, N.Y.: Syracuse University Press, 1984), 50.

43. Ross Lockridge, Jr., *Raintree County*, 211.

44. Ibid., 197.

45. Lutwack, *Role of Place in Literature*, 49.

46. Ibid., 50.

47. Ross Lockridge, Jr., *Raintree County*, 406.

48. Ibid., 926.

49. Ibid., 921.

50. Ibid., 417.

51. Ibid., 408.

52. Ibid., 1053.

53. Ibid.

54. Ibid., 1005.

55. Ibid., 403.

56. Ibid., 402.

57. Ibid., 1052.

58. Ibid., 924.

59. Larry Lockridge, *Shade of the Raintree*, 295.

60. Ibid., 234.

61. Ross Lockridge, Jr., *Raintree County*, 364.

62. Ibid., 1020.

63. Ibid.

64. Ibid., 195.

65. Ibid., 1009.

66. Ibid., 1059.

67. Ibid., 658.

68. Ibid., 258.

69. Ibid., 261.

70. Ibid., 163.

71. Ibid., 153.

72. Ibid., 216.

73. Ibid., 103.

74. Ibid., 406–7.

75. Marguerite Young, *Miss MacIntosh, My Darling* (Normal, Ill.: Dalkey Archive Press, 1993), 77. Originally published by Charles Scribner's Sons, 1965.

76. Ibid., 1002.

77. Ibid., 893.

78. Ibid., 859.

79. Ross Lockridge, Jr., *Raintree County*, 136.

80. Young, *Miss MacIntosh, My Darling*, 158.

81. Ibid., 947.

82. Ibid.

83. Ibid., 272.

84. Ibid., 275.

85. Ibid., 158.

86. Ibid., 75.

87. It might interest the reader to note that the heroes of both novels are Scots.

88. Quoted in Myrtie Barker, "Authoress Young Spins a Long Tale," *Indianapolis News*, 25 October 1965.

89. William Goyen, "A Fable of Illusion and Reality," *New York Times Book Review*, 12 September 1965, p. 5, and Young, *Miss MacIntosh, My Darling*, dust jacket, respectively.

90. *Indianapolis Times*, 30 March 1945.

91. Marguerite Young, *Inviting the Muses: Stories, Essays, Reviews* (Normal, Ill.: Dalkey Archive Press, 1994), 50.

92. Ibid., 145.

93. Ibid., 179.

94. *Indianapolis Times*, 30 March 1945.

95. Young, *Inviting the Muses*, 196.

96. Joseph L. Blotner, "Raintree County Revisited," *The Western Humanities Review* 10 (winter 1955–56): 64.

97. Marthedith Furnas, *A Serpent's Tooth* (New York: Harper and Brothers, 1946), 273.

98. Kurt Vonnegut, Jr., *God Bless You, Mr. Rosewater* (New York: Delacorte Press, 1965), 217.

99. Ibid., 203.

100. Larry Lockridge, *Shade of the Raintree*, 153.

7. That Particular Ground

1. Meredith Nicholson, *A Hoosier Chronicle* (Boston and New York: Houghton Mifflin Company, 1912), 547.

2. Leonard Lutwack, *The Role of Place in Literature* (Syracuse, N.Y.: Syracuse University Press, 1984), 37.

3. Michael Martone, ed., *A Place of Sense: Essays in Search of the Midwest* (Iowa City: The University of Iowa Press, for the Iowa Humanities Board, 1988), 43.

4. Theodore Dreiser, *A Hoosier Holiday* (New York: John Lane Company, 1916), 290.

5. Kurt Vonnegut, Jr., *Fates Worse than Death: An Autobiographical Collage of the 1980s* (New York: G. P. Putnam's Sons, 1991), 125.

6. Ibid., 50.

7. Kurt Vonnegut, Jr., *Cat's Cradle* (New York: Dell Publishing Company, 1963), 66.

8. Ibid., 67.

9. Kurt Vonnegut, Jr., *Slapstick; or, Lonesome No More!* (New York: Bantam Doubleday Dell Publishing Group, 1976), 7.

10. Kurt Vonnegut, Jr., *Breakfast of Champions; or, Goodbye Blue Monday!* (New York: Dell Publishing Company, 1973), 79.

11. Ibid., 196.

12. Dan Wakefield, *Going All the Way* (New York: Delacorte Press, 1970), 51.

13. Susan Neville, *Indiana Winter* (Bloomington and Indianapolis: Indiana University Press, 1994), 32–33.

14. Theodore Dreiser, *Free, and Other Stories* (New York: The Modern Library, 1925), 114. Originally published by Boni and Liveright, 1918.

15. Lutwack, *Role of Place in Literature*, 67.

16. Samuel Yellen, *The Passionate Shepherd: A Book of Stories* (New York: Knopf, 1957), 176.

17. Ibid., 187.

18. Ibid., 53.

19. Ibid., 58.

20. Ibid., 66.

21. Ibid., 186.

22. Ibid.

23. Anna Nicholas, *An Idyl of the Wabash and Other Stories* (Indianapolis and Kansas City: The Bowen-Merrill Company, 1899), 194.

24. Ibid., 178–79.

25. Susan Neville, *The Invention of Flight* (Athens: University of Georgia Press, 1984), 92.

26. Martone, ed., *A Place of Sense*, 31.

27. William Gass, *In the Heart of the Heart of the Country, and Other Stories* (New York: Harper and Row, Publishers, 1968), 181–82.

28. Kurt Vonnegut, Jr., *God Bless You, Mr. Rosewater* (New York: Delacorte Press, 1965), 51.

29. Scott Russell Sanders, *Writing from the Center* (Bloomington and Indianapolis: Indiana University Press, 1995), 49.

30. Ibid., 36.

31. Neville, *Invention of Flight*, 65.

32. Martone, ed., *A Place of Sense*, 31.

33. Lutwack, *Role of Place in Literature*, 40.

34. Ross Lockridge, Jr., *Raintree County* (New York: Penguin Books, 1994), 638.

35. Elizabeth Arthur, *Binding Spell* (New York: Doubleday, 1988), 60.

36. Darryl Pinckney, *High Cotton* (New York: Farrar Straus Giroux, 1992), 55.

37. Wakefield, *Going All the Way*, 21.

38. Lutwack, *Role of Place in Literature*, 44.

39. Ibid., 43.

40. Ibid., 62.

41. Ronald Weber, *The Midwestern Ascendancy in American Writing* (Bloomington and Indianapolis: Indiana University Press, 1992), 39.

42. Sanders, *Writing from the Center*, 37.

43. Weber, *Midwestern Ascendancy in American Writing*, 23.

44. Michael Martone, *Fort Wayne Is Seventh on Hitler's List: Indiana Stories* (Bloomington: Indiana University Press, 1990), 11.

45. Mary Hartwell Catherwood, *The Queen of the Swamp, and Other Plain Americans* (Boston: Houghton Mifflin, 1899), 170. Interestingly, Vonnegut refers to his fiction as "essentially mosaics made up of a whole bunch of tiny chips" in his book *Wampeters, Foma and Granfalloons* (New York: Delacorte Press, 1974), 258.

46. Michael Z. Lewin, *Ask the Right Question* (New York: Putnam, 1971), 20.

47. Ronald Tierney, *The Iron Glove* (New York: St. Martin's Press, 1992), 55, 91.

48. Ronald Tierney, *The Stone Veil* (New York: St. Martin's Press, 1990), 43.

49. Ronald Tierney, *The Steel Web* (New York: St. Martin's Press, 1991), 52.

50. Weber, *Midwestern Ascendancy in American Writing*, 145.

51. Ibid., 1.

52. Marguerite Young, *Miss MacIntosh, My Darling* (Normal, Ill.: Dalkey Archive Press, 1993), 4.

53. Vonnegut, *Fates Worse than Death*, 35.

54. Sanders, *Writing from the Center*, 179.

Bibliography

The literate Hoosier must of course know the Hoosier "classics." Visit the local-interest section of any central Indiana bookstore and you will find the essential titles. But to get a true sense of any Indiana author one must read beyond the canon. An easy way to approach a program of Hoosier literature would be to follow the course of American literature as represented by Hoosier authors.

Begin with Baynard Rush Hall's *The New Purchase*, which can be purchased from Arno Press, New York. It is part of the Mid-American Frontier series. Eunice Beecher's *From Dawn to Daylight* must be read in a library, but it can be read by most people in an afternoon. The central branch of the Indianapolis–Marion County Public Library has several copies, as do the Indiana State Library and the William Henry Smith Memorial Library of the Indiana Historical Society. Not only are these titles the earliest examples of Indiana novels, but they are also useful as sources of frontier Indiana history.

The reader should remember, however, that the more typical form of fiction of this era was the short story and the serials that appeared in popular periodicals. With that in mind, the reader would do well to read Mary Hartwell Catherwood's stories, most easily accessible in the collection *Queen of the Swamp, and Other Plain Americans*, which can be checked out of many public libraries, and Edward Eggleston's *The Hoosier School-Master*, which first appeared serially, but which can be picked up in any Indiana bookstore.

Next the reader should begin to explore the Hoosier romancers. As a bridge from early realism to romance, one might begin with Maurice Thompson's collection *Hoosier Mosaics* because it is so like Catherwood's stories and so unlike Thompson's later and more popular work. Then read his *Alice of Old Vincennes* by way of comparison. Also for purposes of contrast the reader should glance through Catherwood's *The Romance of Dollard* or *Lazarre*. A glance will probably suffice.

Next on the agenda would be Charles Major's *When Knighthood Was in Flower* and George Barr McCutcheon's *Graustark*, nearly perfect examples of the historical romance genre. Unless the reader is totally captivated by the latter, he or she can in good conscience skip the rest of the Graustarkian novels of McCutcheon. A must read, however, is Major's *Bears of Blue River* for all the reasons discussed in the text. Move on to Tarkington's *Monsieur Beaucaire* and *The Gentleman from Indiana*. *Beaucaire* will probably engage the contemporary reader only for its historical interest; it is not nearly as palatable as *When Knighthood Was in Flower*. But *Gentleman* is enjoyable on its own merits and is indispensable before reading the rest of Tarkington.

Now the reader can begin to explore Meredith Nicholson's *The House of a Thousand Candles* and *A Hoosier Chronicle*, these two being the most important titles with which to familiarize oneself. The rest of Nicholson's novels can be sampled at random for a fair representation of this author's fiction. It is useful, however, to read some of his essays in collections such as *The Hoosiers* and *Old Familiar Faces* for additional insight into both Nicholson and his contemporaries, and the Hoosier literary scene. Read Gene Stratton-Porter's *A Girl of the Limberlost* at this juncture for its intentional and effective use of an Indiana setting for a romance novel, but save the rest of Stratton-Porter for later reading.

Finally, return to McCutcheon. No Hoosier should begin and end his or her consideration of George Barr McCutcheon with *Graustark*. Without reading both *Viola Gwyn* and *The Sherrods* the reader will have missed out on McCutcheon's best work and two wonderful examples of early realism.

Those two novels will be a good transition to the social history novels of Tarkington and to Dreiser and his contribution to naturalism. One should read Tarkington's *Growth* trilogy in its entirety. *The Turmoil* and *The Magnificent Ambersons* are still in print. *Alice Adams*, a delightful novel that begins to probe the phenomenon of working women in the new industrial society, is still in print. After *Alice* it would be appropriate to read Dreiser's *Sister Carrie* and *Jennie Gerhardt* for a darker image of the class system and the socioeconomic condition of women, as well as for Dreiser's markedly different perspective on the Indiana of his youth. The reader should also experience David Graham Phillips's *Susan Lenox*. It is a lengthy book, but well worth the effort, as a strong portrait of the "new woman" and as Phillips's magnum opus, not to mention the fact that its Indiana setting figures rather prominently early in the book. For more insight into Dreiser, *The "Genius"* is useful, and it might be interesting to explore Dreiser's own trilogy of industrialism and materialism—*The Financier*, *The Titan*, and *The Stoic*—and compare Dreiser's take on the issues with Tarkington's. Finish with *An American Tragedy*.

Before the reader begins a study of rural literature it would be helpful to read Roy W. Meyer's *The Middle Western Farm Novel in the Twentieth Century*, published by the University of Nebraska Press, 1965, though it is certainly not necessary to a thorough appreciation of LeRoy MacLeod's two Indiana farm novels, *The Years of Peace* and *The Crowded Hill*. MacLeod's first novel, *Three Steeples: A Tragedy of Earth*, is not as satisfying, though it is set in rural Indiana. I found these novels only in the Indiana State Library.

The reader can now enjoy Gene Stratton-Porter to his or her heart's content. Begin with the earlier romances—*Freckles*, *Laddie*, *The Harvester*—all of which can be purchased, and then move into Stratton-Porter's later phase, paying particular attention to *A Daughter of the Land* and *The White Flag*. The latter was her most realistic novel and probably her least popular.

By now the reader should be ready, if not eager, to tackle the two giants of Indiana literature, *Raintree County* and *Miss MacIntosh, My Darling*. The former should be read in its entirety along with Larry Lockridge's *Shade of the Raintree: The Life and Death of Ross Lockridge, Jr.*, which will help the reader enormously in digesting the novel. *Miss MacIntosh* can be picked up and sampled randomly as one might a book of poetry because of the lack of a discernible narrative structure, and it can be appreciated even on a piecemeal level for its sheer lyric beauty. One should not limit one's exposure to Marguerite Young to the novel, however. *Angel in the Forest* is a most engaging and impressionistic exploration of the

New Harmony experiment, and her poetry is worth exploring as well.

Before one moves into contemporary literature and the theme of place one could not do better than to read Leonard Lutwack's marvelous *The Role of Place in Literature*, published by Syracuse University Press in 1984. For a more geographically focused analysis of "place value," *A Place of Sense: Essays in Search of the Midwest*, edited by Michael Martone, is very useful. Every literate Hoosier should read as much Vonnegut as he/she can read if for no other reason than to get some sense of Indiana's most popular, enigmatic, and well-known literary figure. One should read representative samplings of Dan Wakefield, Michael Martone, Nancy N. Baxter, and James Alexander Thom, particularly Thom's *Long Knife* as a historically accurate counterbalance to the George Rogers Clark that appears in *Alice of Old Vincennes*, and the delightful novels of Elizabeth Arthur, Darryl Pinckney, and Don Kurtz. And finally, one should read Susan Neville and Scott Russell Sanders extensively.

In addition, the reader must not forget the novels of Jessamyn West and Margaret Weymouth Jackson. And every Hoosier worth his literary salt should have read the short stories of George Ade and Wallace's *Ben-Hur*.

In terms of secondary sources and biographies I have chosen to mention only those I found to be the most consistently useful to the casual reader. An absolute "must read" is Ronald Weber's *The Midwestern Ascendancy in American Writing* published in 1992 by Indiana University Press. It is indispensable for a thorough introduction to midwestern literature in its broader historical context. It will disappoint Hoosiers somewhat because it does not perhaps give Indiana its due and, in some respects, this book has been a feeble and far inferior attempt to rectify that, or at least to expand the Hoosier story for a local audience. Arthur Shumaker's *A History of Indiana Literature* is an invaluable reference, as is *Indiana Authors and Their Books*, compiled by R. E. Banta. For individual genres, Blanche Housman Gelfant's *The American City Novel*, is still useful for an introduction to the subject, as is Roy W. Meyer's *The Middle Western Farm Novel* mentioned earlier.

For lesser novels of interest to readers who want to explore various subjects in Indiana literature, there are a couple of novels about New Harmony: Robert Dale Owen's *Beyond the Breakers* and Caroline Dale Snedeker's *Seth Way*. For novels about the Civil War and/or Morgan's Raid there are *The Legionaries* by Millard F. Cox, Caroline Krout's *Knights in Fustian*, Frederick Landis's *The Glory of His Country*, *A Knight of the Golden Circle* by Ulysses S. Lesh, and *The Test of Loyalty* by James M. Hiatt.

Index